CW01459514

This book belongs to:

_____

CASEY CROSSBAR

EXTRA! BONUS!

"Find your extra FREE bonus at the start of the solutions section!"

Copyright Notice

Copyright © 2025 Casey Crossbar.
All rights reserved.
This book is for personal use only. Please do not copy, reproduce, distribute, or share the blank pages in any form—digitally or physically —without written permission.

FOOTBALL WORDSEARCH #1

Get ready to score! Find all the football words hidden in the puzzle. Keep your eyes sharp and kick off the search!

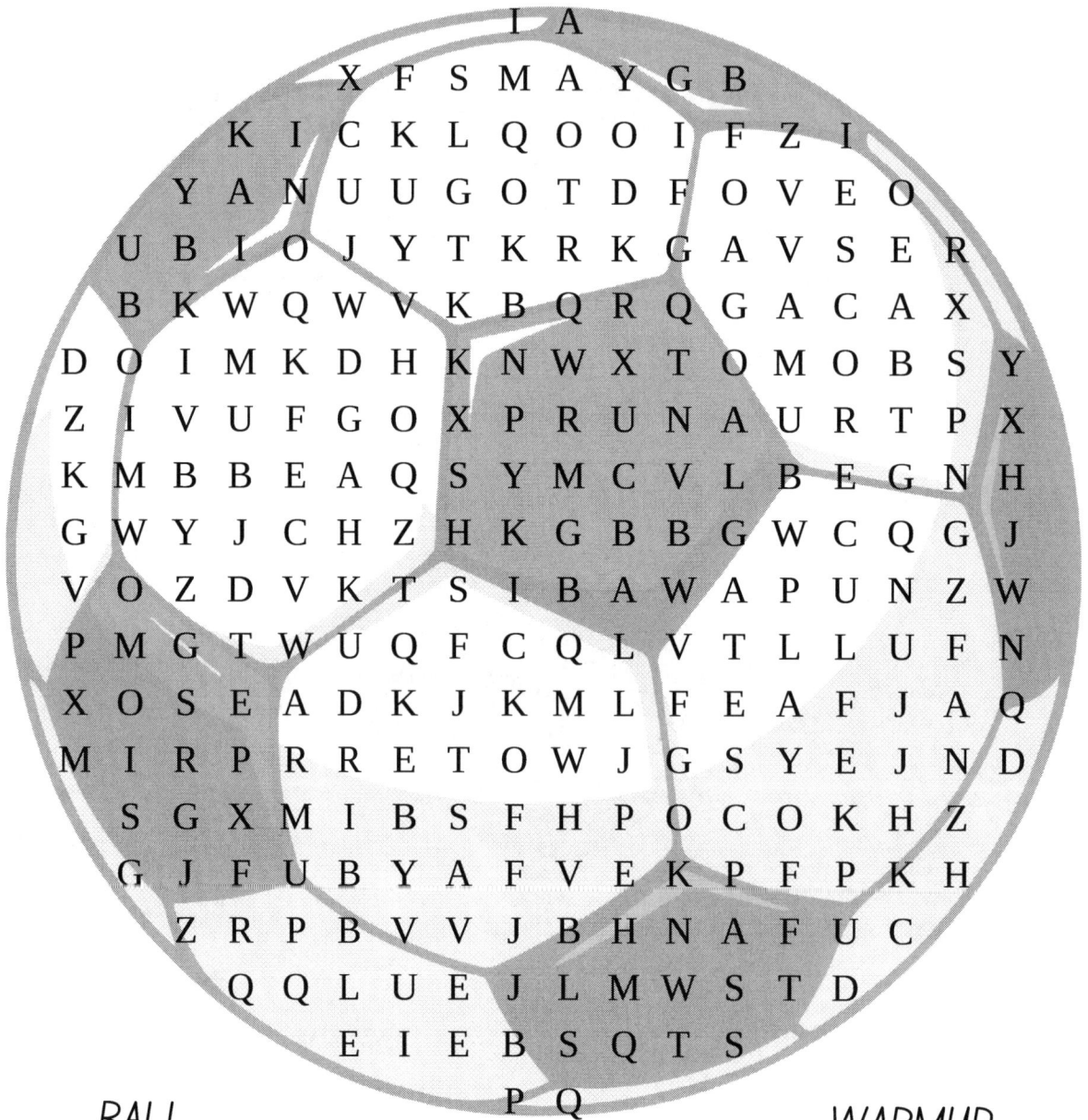

```
            I A
          X F S M A Y G B
        K I C K L Q O O I F Z I
        Y A N U U G O T D F O V E O
        U B I O J Y T K R K G A V S E R
        B K W Q W V K B Q R Q G A C A X
      D O I M K D H K N W X T O M O B S Y
      Z I V U F G O X P R U N A U R T P X
      K M B B E A Q S Y M C V L B E G N H
      G W Y J C H Z H K G B B G W C Q G J
      V O Z D V K T S I B A W A P U N Z W
      P M G T W U Q F C Q L V T L L U F N
      X O S E A D K J K M L F E A F J A Q
      M I R P R E T O W J G S Y E J N D
        S G X M I B S F H P O C O K H Z
        G J F U B Y A T F V E K P F P K H
          Z R P B V V J B H N A F U C
            Q Q L U E J L M W S T D
              E I E B S Q T S
                  P Q
```

BALL		WARMUP
KICK	DRIBBLE	GOAL
PLAYOFF	KICKOFF	PASS
SCORE	RUN	SAVE

FOOTBALL FACTS

Most Premier League Appearances:

Gareth Barry holds the record for the most Premier League appearances, playing 653 matches between 1998 and 2018.

Most Own Goals in Premier League History:

Richard Dunne holds the record for the most own goals in Premier League history, with 10 across his career.

KICKOFF CRYPTOGRAM CHALLENGE! #1

Use the clues in the legend to match letters and reveal the secret football phrase!

A	B	C	D	E	F	G	H	I	J	K	L	M

N	O	P	Q	R	S	T	U	V	W	X	Y	Z

1. PASS , SHOOT

SHOOT SCORE !

Hint: Three steps to winning the game!

2. DRIBBLE TO

VICTORY !

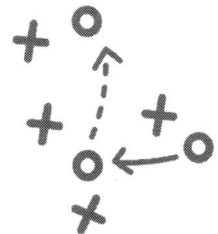

Hint: Take the ball all the way!

THE FOOTBALL MAZE RUN #1

Help both players dribble their way to the goal and score!

FOOTBALL QUIZ

1 - Which footballer is often referred to as 'CR7'?

A) Cristiano Ronaldo
B) Carlos Ruiz
C) Cesc Fàbregas
D) César Azpilicueta

2 - How many times has Lionel Messi won the Ballon d'Or as of 2024?

A) 5
B) 7
C) 8
D) 9

3 - Who is the youngest goalscorer in a World Cup tournament?

A) Kylian Mbappé
B) Pelé
C) Michael Owen
D) Diego Maradona

4 - Which English club holds the record for the longest unbeaten run in the Premier League?

A) Liverpool
B) Manchester City
C) Chelsea
D) Arsenal

WOULD YOU RATHER?

Would you rather be the fastest player on the field or the strongest?

....

Would you rather play a football match in the pouring rain or in the blazing heat?

....

Would you rather be the goalkeeper who saves the winning penalty or the striker who scores the winning goal?

....

Would you rather wear a football kit that's too big or boots that are too tight?

....

Would you rather be known for your amazing dribbling skills or your powerful long-range shots?

....

WORD UNSCRAMBLE #1

RAYHR NAKE

_ _ _ _ _   _ _ _ _

CLANED ECIR

_ _ _ _ _ _   _ _ _ _

LEOC PELARM

_ _ _ _   _ _ _ _ _ _

HILP NEDFO

_ _ _ _   _ _ _ _ _

BAYKUO KAAS

_ _ _ _ _ _   _ _ _ _

FOOTBALL WORDSEARCH #2

```
                          C G E
                        R B O O T S
                      T E A M M A T E
                      B S H W K N B R
        V M D E X   G I R Y I L W M
        T E A M W O R K Z H Q S Q T
        T D N M G T     W N U Z K
        H X E Q C             N
        R T C               D N T
        R K Q I           R U K X F
      E Q P W Z T         A P E W M
        Y Q Z N I       F M D A D G C
        B F Q Y O U T H D M D D P M
        H X G O A L K E E P E R I C
      C L U B E Q M K H N O W Z T O S
        H I L M Y D L M Z B O C A P
        P R A C T I C E E X Z H C
        U T H J E R S E Y A H
              L R H Y T X
```

BOOTS   CLUB   COACH
GOALKEEPER   JERSEY   PITCH
PRACTICE   TEAMMATE   TEAMWORK
YOUTH

SOLVE THESE RIDDLES

#1 - I protect you from kicks and blows on the field, worn under socks and never revealed. I'm hard on the outside, soft on the skin, keeping your legs safe while you win. What am I?

#2 - I wear a special band on my arm, leading my team with strength and charm. I make decisions, guide the play, and inspire the team every match day. Who am I?

#3 - I stretch behind posts to catch what flies through, a target for players to aim and pursue. When I ripple, the crowd may cheer; without me, balls would disappear. What am I?

#4 - I start and stop the game's flow, a short sharp sound to let players know. In the hands of one who controls the play, my signal can change the course of the day. What am I?

KICKOFF CRYPTOGRAM CHALLENGE! #2

Use the clues in the legend to match letters and reveal the secret football phrase!

A	B	C	D	E	F	G	H	I	J	K	L	M
whistle	checkered flag	net	corner flag	sock	goal	boot	gloves	first aid	FC pennant	shorts	megaphone	card

N	O	P	Q	R	S	T	U	V	W	X	Y	Z
flag	clipboard	in/out	shoe	ball	GOAL	stopwatch	scarf	cone	pitch	boot+ball	7:0	jersey

GOAL!!!

1.

[B E L I E V E]   [I N]

[Y O U R]   [T E A M] !

Hint: Trust your mates on the pitch!

2.

[B A C K]   [O F]   [T H E]

   [N E T] !

Hint: Where the ball goes when you score!

THE FOOTBALL MAZE RUN #2

You're late for training! Get to the pitch quickly.

FOOTBALL FACTS

First International Match:

The first-ever international football match was played between Scotland and England in 1872, ending in a 0-0 draw.

First Woman Referee at Men's World Cup:

Stéphanie Frappart made history as the first female referee to officiate a men's FIFA World Cup match in 2022.

WORD UNSCRAMBLE #2

Hint - Popular Footballers

NELLIO MISSE

_ _ _ _ _ _   _ _ _ _ _

IANLYK BAMPEP

_ _ _ _ _ _   _ _ _ _ _

RINGEL HANDLAA

_ _ _ _ _ _   _ _ _ _ _ _ _

ROADNLO

_ _ _ _ _ _ _

MARYEN

_ _ _ _ _ _

FOOTBALL WORDSEARCH #3

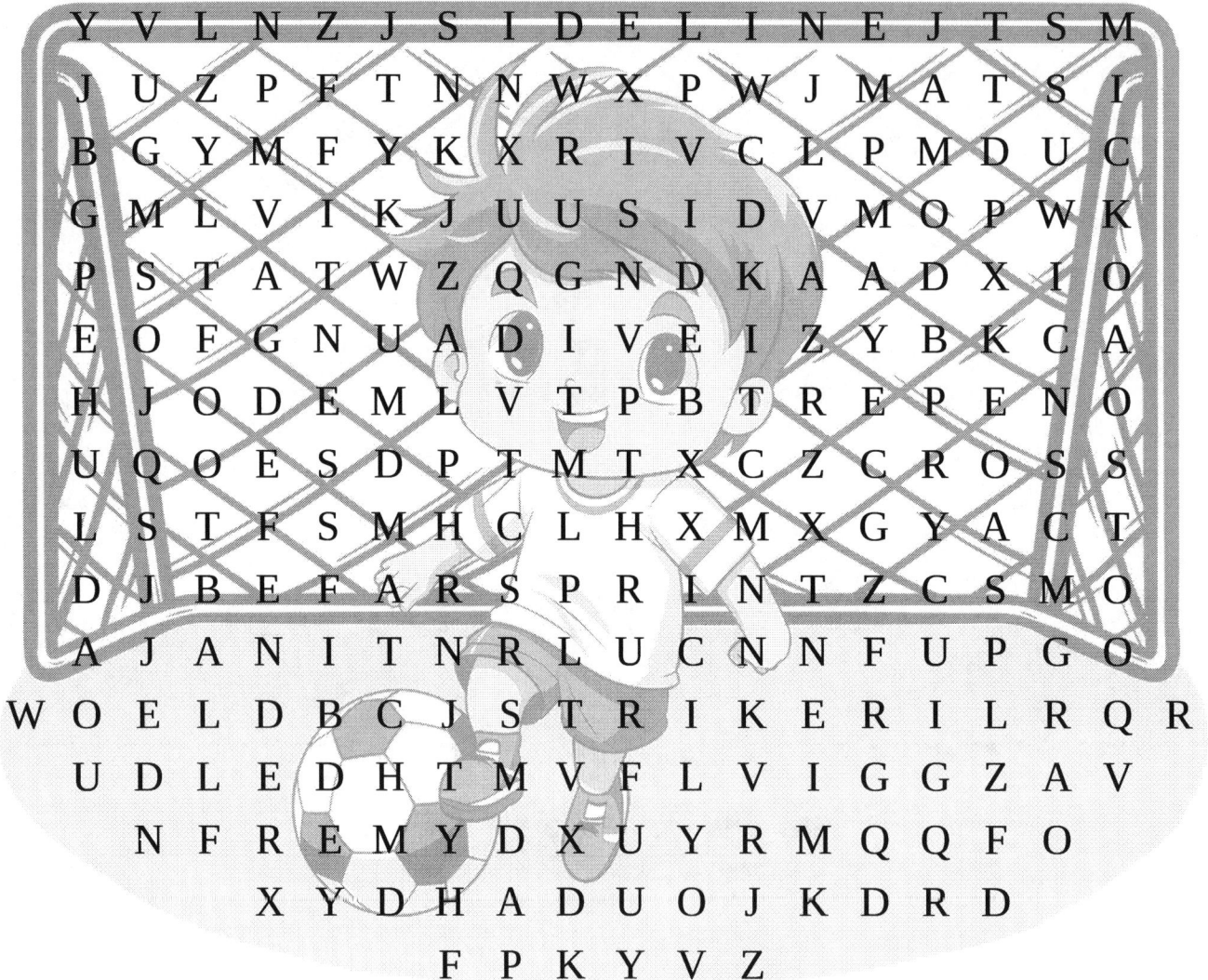

```
Y V L N Z J S I D E L I N E J T S M
J U Z P F T N N W X P W J M A T S I
B G Y M F Y K X R I V C L P M D U C
G M L V I K J U U S I D V M O P W K
P S T A T W Z Q G N D K A A D X I O
E O F G N U A D I V E I Z Y B K C A
H J O D E M L V T P B T R E P E N O
U Q O E S D P T M T X C Z C R O S S
L S T F S M H C L H X M X G Y A C T
D J B E F A R S P R I N T Z C S M O
A J A N I T N R L U C N N F U P G O
W O E L D B C J S T R I K E R I L R Q R
U D L E D H T M V F L V I G G Z A V
N F R E M Y D X U Y R M Q Q F O
X Y D H A D U O J K D R D
F P K Y V Z
```

CROSS   DEFENDER   DIVE

FITNESS   FOOTBALL   KIT

MATCH   SIDELINE   SPRINT

STRIKER

THE FOOTBALL MAZE RUN #3

The team's down by one! Reach the scoreboard and even the score!

SCORE
1-2

WOULD YOU RATHER?

Would you rather never lose a match but never score a goal, or score a goal every game but never win?

....

Would you rather play for your country and miss a penalty in the world cup final or win every game for your local club but never get recognised?

....

Would you rather be known as a fair player but never win trophies or be known as a rule-breaker and win everything?

....

Would you rather play for your favorite team and earn just enough pocket money for snacks or play for a team you don't like at all but become one of the richest players in the league?

....

Would you rather take every penalty kick for your team or every free kick?

....

FOOTBALL QUIZ

5 - What do you call a match played between two teams from the same city?

A) Friendly match
B) El Clásico
C) Derby match
D) Exhibition game

6 - Who won the 2022 FIFA World Cup?

A) Argentina
B) France
C) Germany
D) Brazil

7 - Which player scored the 'Hand of God' goal?

A) Lionel Messi
B) Cristiano Ronaldo
C) Diego Maradona
D) Zinedine Zidane

8 - Which club did David Beckham play for after leaving Manchester United?

A) Real Madrid
B) LA Galaxy
C) Paris Saint-Germain
D) AC Milan

FOOTBALL WORDSEARCH #4

```
                        F R
        Y P K Y H S B W L D
        T G N F N L E F K K
N L F P R J Q N N L Q G F G N R J C J N
R R G S D C N E T Y S W I S V E L E D X
M A N A G E R F A N S V T A F O U L F C
J P O I N T S T T O T L A B B A S Y U A
Z X W R M G U V Z P H G C Q P L H Z L S
O D L L O G X L M C W Z K M V M I Q L A
F K R R J O Y D H H Z T L F E O N M T B
L H C G D Z O F C M G C E L M S P I I I
M G X S T A N D S Q R C N F D X A A M R
D S W Y F Y G S T D A O L X N V D X E T
A R F Q D V O P V G S H F B H H M W Z X
J O G K O M Z T S X S U O D T I U M X H
O N Z Z Q U I I J T O X T G W M O T X P
```

FANS   FOUL   FULLTIME
GRASS   MANAGER   NET
POINTS   SHINPAD   STANDS
TACKLE

KICKOFF CRYPTOGRAM CHALLENGE! #3

Use the clues in the legend to match letters and reveal the secret football phrase!

A	B	C	D	E	F	G	H	I	J	K	L	M
👟	whistle	7:0	megaphone	jersey	pitch	stopwatch	shorts	clipboard	goal	ball	flag	net

N	O	P	Q	R	S	T	U	V	W	X	Y	Z
kit	boot	IN/OUT	scarf	shoe	sock	flag	gloves	cone	card	GOAL	flag	FC

1.

KEEP YOUR EYE

ON THE BALL !

Hint: Watch closely, don't lose sight of the ball!

2.

GIVE IT YOUR

BEST SHOT !

Hint: Try as hard as you can!

FOOTBALL FACTS

Most Goals in a World Cup:

Just Fontaine holds the record for the most goals scored in a single World Cup, with 13 goals for France in 1958.

First Player to Win Three World Cups:

Brazilian Pelé is the only player to have won three World Cups (1958, 1962, and 1970). (As of 2024)

THE FOOTBALL MAZE RUN #4

Help the top player find his way to his teammate so they can play football together!

FOOTBALL WORDSEARCH #5

Get ready to score! Find all the football words hidden in the puzzle. Keep your eyes sharp and kick off the search!

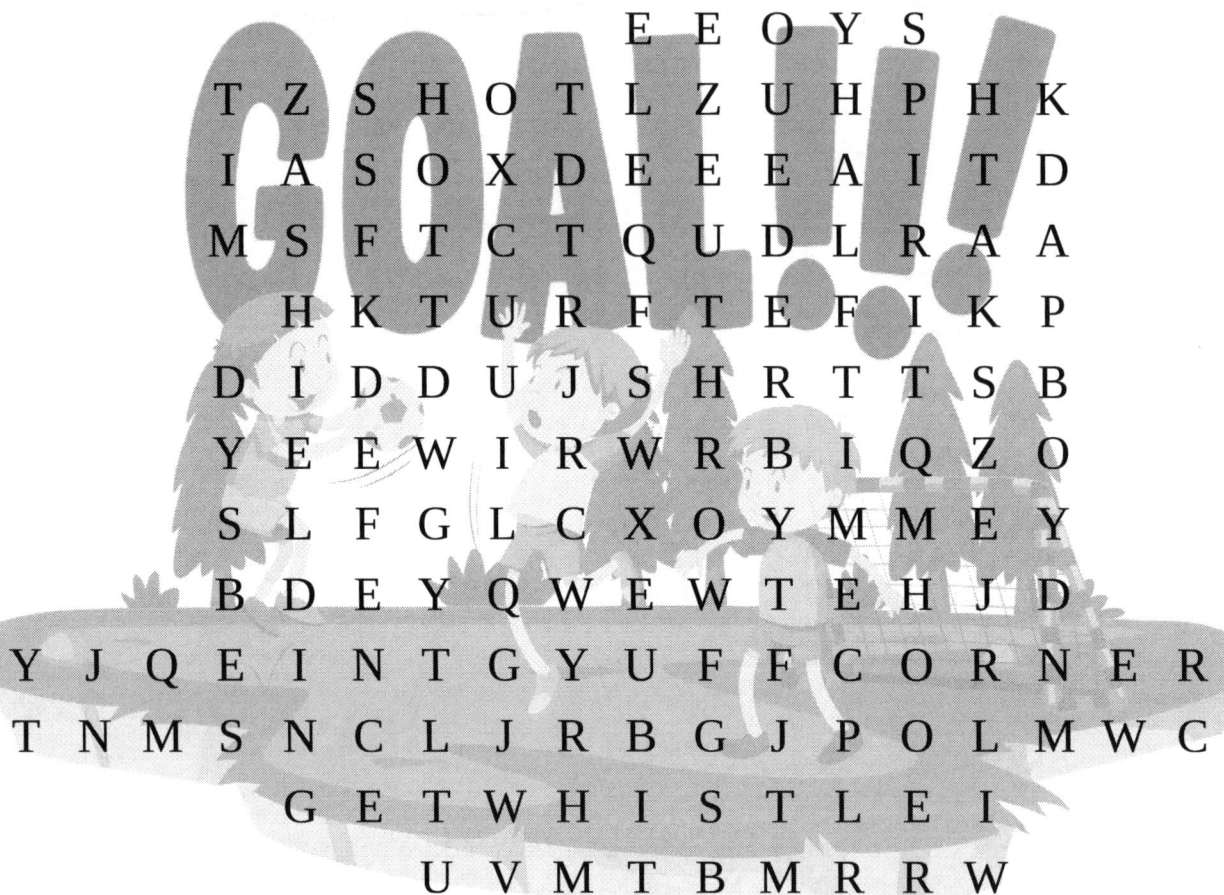

```
        E E O Y S
  T Z S H O T L Z U H P H K
  I A S O X D E E E A I T D
  M S F T C T Q U D L R A A
    H K T U R F T E F I K P
  D I D D U J S H R T T S B
  Y E E W I R W R B I Q Z O
  S L F G L C X O Y M M E Y
    B D E Y Q W E W T E H J D
  Y J Q E I N T G Y U F F C O R N E R
  T N M S N C L J R B G J P O L M W C
      G E T W H I S T L E I
      U V M T B M R R W
```

CORNER	SHIELDING	DERBY
HALFTIME	DEFENCE	SHOT
SPIRIT	THROW	TURF
WHISTLE		

WORD UNSCRAMBLE #3

Hint - National Football Teams

LANEGND

_ _ _ _ _ _ _

BARLIZ

_ _ _ _ _ _

PANJA

_ _ _ _ _

GERINIA

_ _ _ _ _ _ _

CERFAN

_ _ _ _ _ _

DESIGN YOUR ULTIMATE PLAYER

"Pick the best abilities from your favourite players to create your ultimate player! Fill in their names for each attribute."

Vision

Footballing Intelligence

Strength

Passion

Work Rate

Speed

Passing Accuracy

Shooting

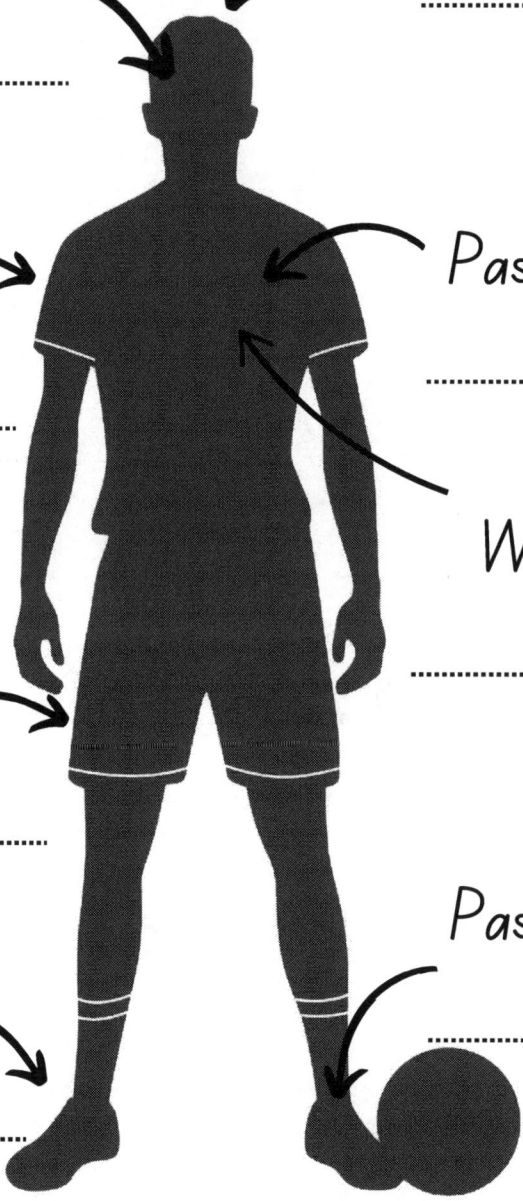

THE FOOTBALL MAZE RUN #5

Lead the players to reach the trophy stand after winning a match, avoiding obstacles like fans, photographers, and barriers.

KICKOFF CRYPTOGRAM CHALLENGE! #4

Use the clues in the legend to match letters and reveal the secret football phrase!

A	B	C	D	E	F	G	H	I	J	K	L	M
🧤	🥅	🏁	🧦	🚩	🧰	🔺	GOAL	FC	👕	📣	👟	📋

N	O	P	Q	R	S	T	U	V	W	X	Y	Z
🥅	🧣	⬜	🚩	📣	👟	⏱	IN/OUT	🟨	⚽	🔢	👟	🩳

1.

PLAY LIKE A

CHAMPION !

Hint: Give your best effort on the pitch!

2.

WINNERS NEVER

QUIT !

Hint: Winners keep trying, no matter what!

HOME   AWAY

TIME

FOOTBALL QUIZ

9 - Which national team won the first-ever FIFA World Cup in 1930?

A) Argentina
B) Uruguay
C) Brazil
D) Germany

10 - Who won the Golden Boot at the 2018 FIFA World Cup?

A) Kylian Mbappé
B) Luka Modrić
C) Harry Kane
D) Antoine Griezmann

11 - Which club is nicknamed 'The Gunners'?

A) Manchester City
B) Chelsea FC
C) Arsenal FC
D) Liverpool FC

12 - What does VAR stand for in football?

A) Video Assistance Review
B) Video Assistant Referee
C) Virtual Action Replay
D) Verified Authority Referee

DESIGN YOUR OWN TEAM

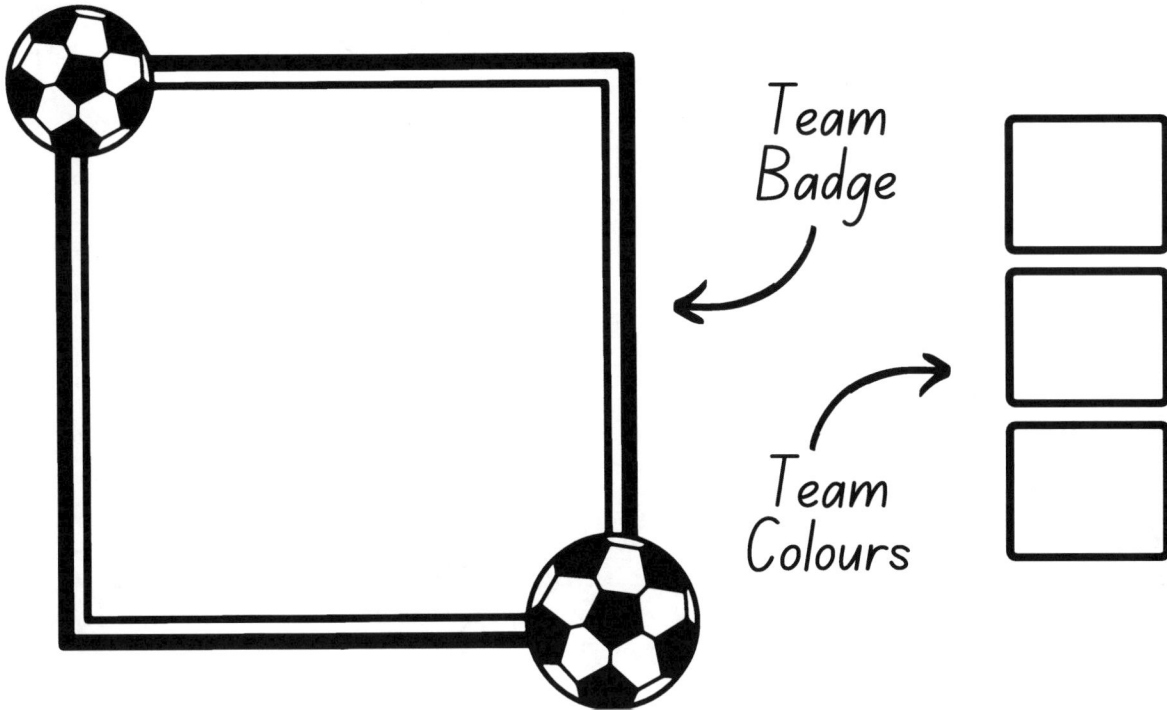

Team Badge

Team Colours

TEAM NAME: ....

TEAM NICKNAME: ....

FOUNDED: .... **STADIUM CAPACITY:** ....

STADIUM NAME: ....

KIT SPONSOR: ....

TEAM FORMATION: ....

TEAM MOTTO: ....

MANAGER: ....

FOOTBALL WORDSEARCH #6

Get ready to score! Find all the football words hidden in the puzzle. Keep your eyes sharp and kick off the search!

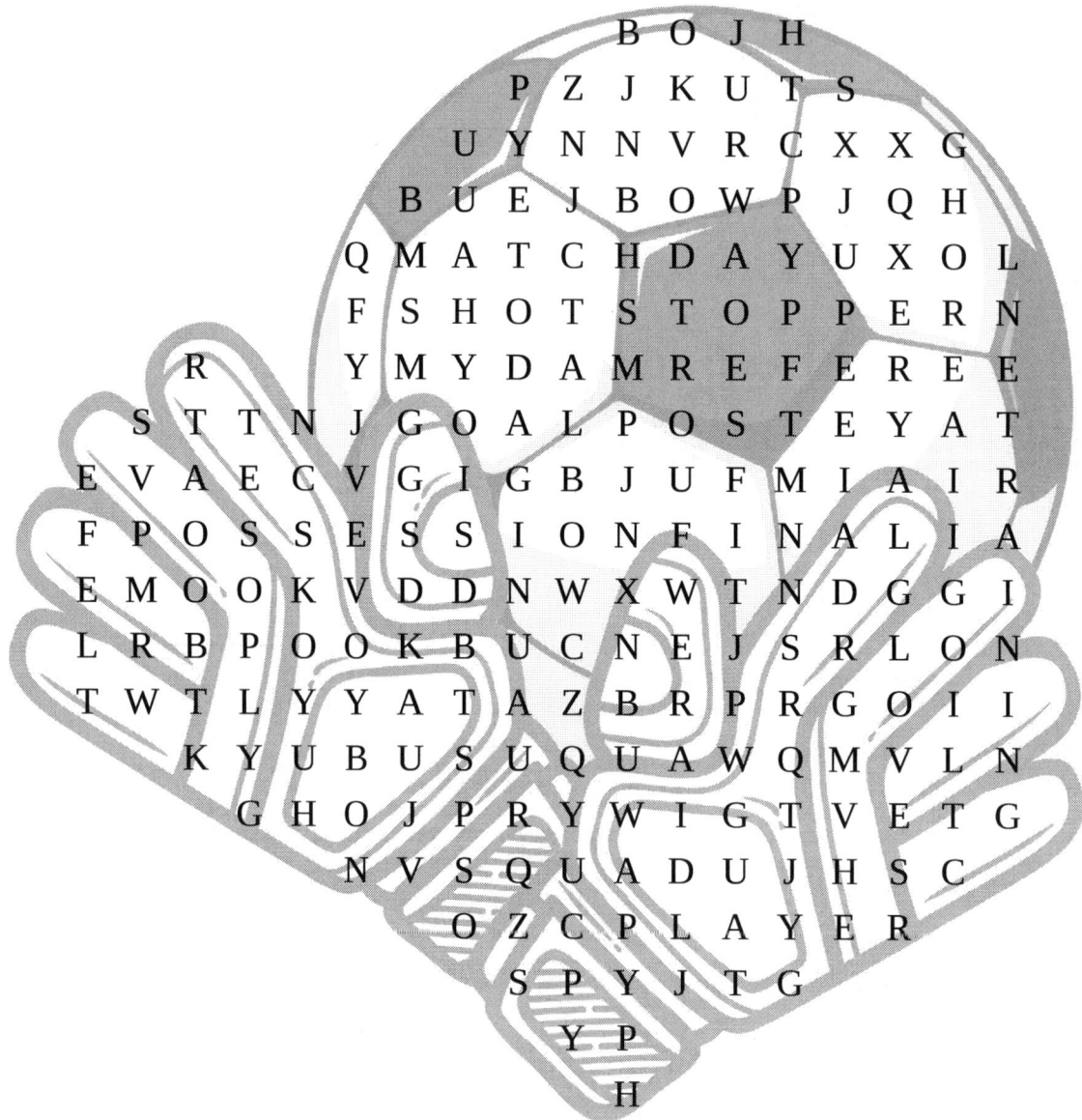

```
            B O J H
          P Z J K U T S
        U Y N N V R C X X G
      B U E J B O W P J Q H
    Q M A T C H D A Y U X O L
    F S H O T S T O P P E R N
  R   Y M Y D A M R E F E R E E
  S T T N J G O A L P O S T E Y A T
  E V A E C V G I G B J U F M I A I R
  F P O S S E S S I O N F I N A L I A
  E M O O K V D D N W X W T N D G G I
  L R B P O O K B U C N E J S R L O N
  T W T L Y Y A T A Z B R P R G O I I
  K Y U B U S U Q U A W Q M V L N
  G H O J P R Y W I G T V E T G
    N V S Q U A D U J H S C
      O Z C P L A Y E R
        S P Y J T G
          Y P
          H
```

FINAL	GLOVES	GOALPOST
MATCHDAY	PLAYER	POSSESSION
REFEREE	SHOTSTOPPER	SQUAD
TRAINING		

FOOTBALL QUIZ

13 - Which Italian club has won the most Serie A titles?

A) AC Milan
B) Juventus
C) Inter Milan
D) Roma

14 - What is the nickname of the Italian national football team?

A) La Roja
B) Die Mannschaft
C) Azzurri
D) Les Bleus

15 - Which of these players has scored the fastest hat-trick in Premier League history?

A) Thierry Henry
B) Sadio Mane
C) Sergio Agüero
D) Mohamed Salah

16 - Which footballer was nicknamed 'El Fenómeno'?

A) Ronaldinho
B) Romário
C) Ronaldo Nazário
D) Rivaldo

THE FOOTBALL MAZE RUN #6

Navigate the player's car through a traffic-filled maze to make it to the stadium in time.

SCORE
1-2

KICKOFF CRYPTOGRAM CHALLENGE! #5

Use the clues in the legend to match letters and reveal the secret football phrase!

A	B	C	D	E	F	G	H	I	J	K	L	M

N	O	P	Q	R	S	T	U	V	W	X	Y	Z

1.

F O O T B A L L   I S

L I F E !

Hint: For true fans, this sport means everything!

2.

T H E   C R O W D

G O E S   W I L D !

Hint: Everyone's cheering loudly!

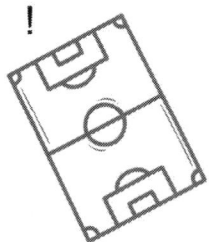

FOOTBALL FACTS

Most Games Managed in the Premier League:

Arsène Wenger managed 828 Premier League games with Arsenal, making him the manager with the most matches in the competition.

Most Popular Sport in the World:

Football is the most popular sport globally, with over 3 billion fans worldwide.

FOOTBALL WORDSEARCH #7

Get ready to score! Find all the football words hidden in the puzzle. Keep your eyes sharp and kick off the search!

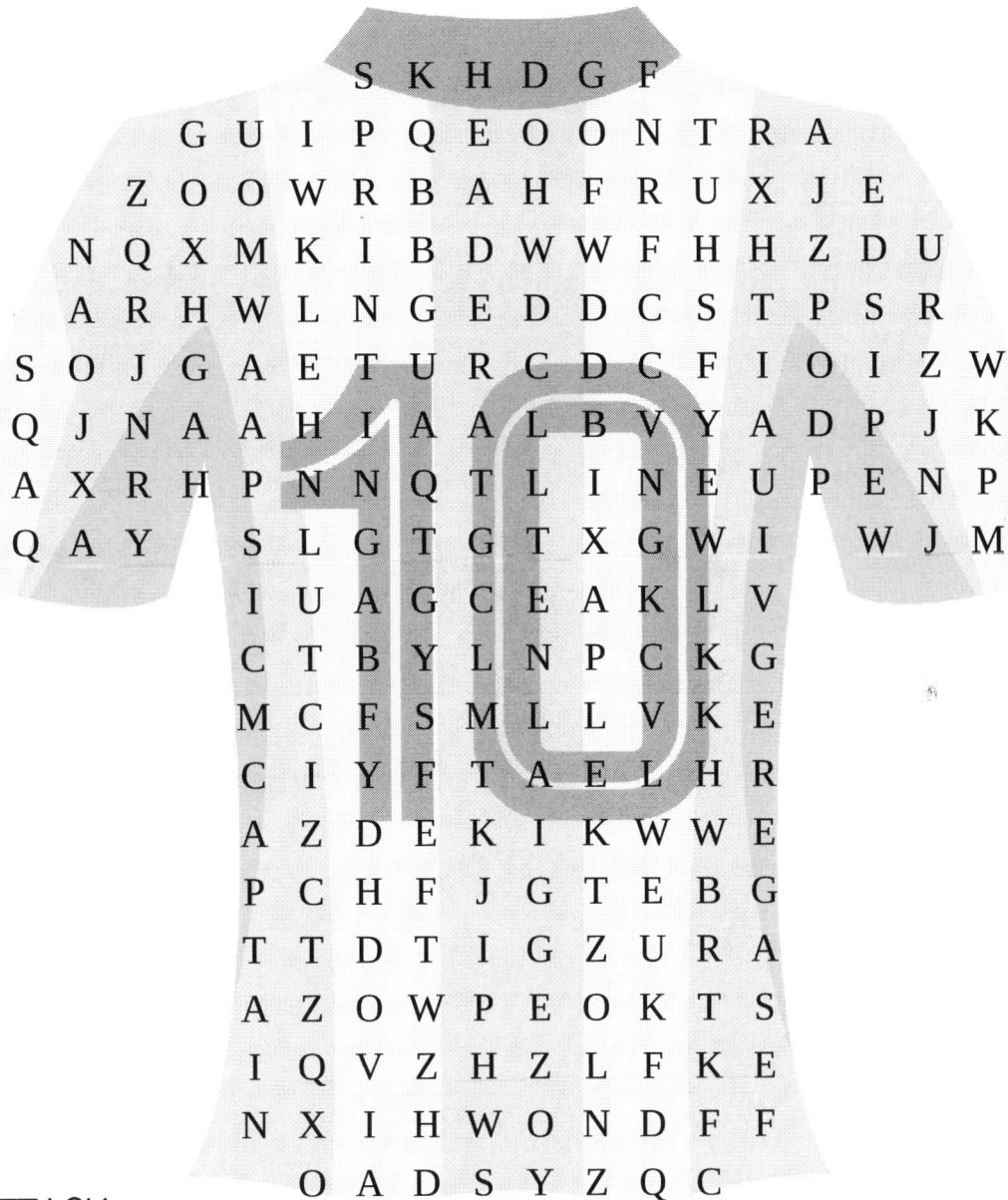

```
        S K H D G F
    G U I P Q E O O N T R A
    Z O O W R B A H F R U X J E
  N Q X M K I B D W W F H H Z D U
  A R H W L N G E D D C S T P S R
  S O J G A E T U R C D C F I O I Z W
  Q J N A A H I A A L B V Y A D P J K
  A X R H P N N Q T L I N E U P E N P
  Q A Y   S L G T G T X G W I   W J M
        I U A G C E A K L V
        C T B Y L N P C K G
        M C F S M L L V K E
        C I Y F T A E L H R
        A Z D E K I K W W E
        P C H F J G T E B G
        T T D T I G Z U R A
        A Z O W P E O K T S
        I Q V Z H Z L F K E
        N X I H W O N D F F
        O A D S Y Z Q C
```

ATTACK
HEADER
OFFSIDE
SUBSTITUTE

CAPTAIN
LINEUP
PLAYMAKER

CROSSFIELD
MIDFIELD
SPRINTING

CAN YOU PREDICT THE FUTURE?

Which team do you think will win the UEFA Women's Champions League in the 2025/2026 season?

....

Which team do you think will win the Women's FA Cup in 2026?

....

Which country do you think will win the Women's World Cup 2027 tournament?

....

Who do you think will win the Women's Ballon d'Or in 2026?

....

Which Women's team will finish higher in the La Liga Table: Barcelona or Real Madrid?   (2025/2026 season)

....

THE FOOTBALL MAZE RUN #7

Race through the maze
to sign a professional contract!

KICKOFF CRYPTOGRAM CHALLENGE! #6

Use the clues in the legend to match letters and reveal the secret football phrase!

A	B	C	D	E	F	G	H	I	J	K	L	M
🚩	GOAL	🏁	⏱	🥅	🎺	FC	👟	🧰	🧦	📢	7:0	🩳

N	O	P	Q	R	S	T	U	V	W	X	Y	Z
📋	🥅	⚽field	🧤	👟	👟	⚽	🏳	👕	IN/OUT	🧣	🔺	🟨

1.

ON THE WAY TO

WEMBLEY !

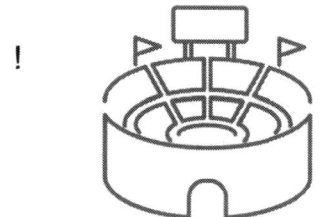

Hint: Heading to the most famous stadium!

2.

RISE TO THE

CHALLENGE !

Hint: Step up and give it your all!

FILL YOUR TROPHY CABINET

Trophy Ideas

FOOTBALL QUIZ

17 - Which country won the first Women's World Cup in 1991?

A) Norway
B) Germany
C) USA
D) China

18 - What is the name of Real Madrid's stadium?

A) Camp Nou
B) Santiago Bernabéu
C) Wanda Metropolitano
D) Mestalla

19 - Which player has the record for the most goals scored in a single Premier League season (as of 2025)?

A) Mohamed Salah
B) Alan Shearer
C) Erling Haaland
D) Thierry Henry

20 - What year did England win the FIFA World Cup?

A) 1966
B) 1970
C) 1986
D) 1990

FOOTBALL QUIZ

21 - Which club did Kylian Mbappé play for before joining Paris Saint-Germain (PSG)?

A) Lyon
B) Marseille
C) AS Monaco
D) Lille

22 - Which Premier League club is known for having a 'claret and blue' kit alongside West Ham United?

A) Aston Villa
B) Crystal Palace
C) Newcastle United
D) Southampton

23 - What animal is featured on the badge of Leicester City?

A) Lion
B) Fox
C) Eagle
D) Wolf

24 - What is the nickname of Newcastle United?

A) The Magpies
B) The Foxes
C) The Eagles
D) The Hammers

THE FOOTBALL MAZE RUN #8

The referee lost his whistle! Help him find it before the big match begins!

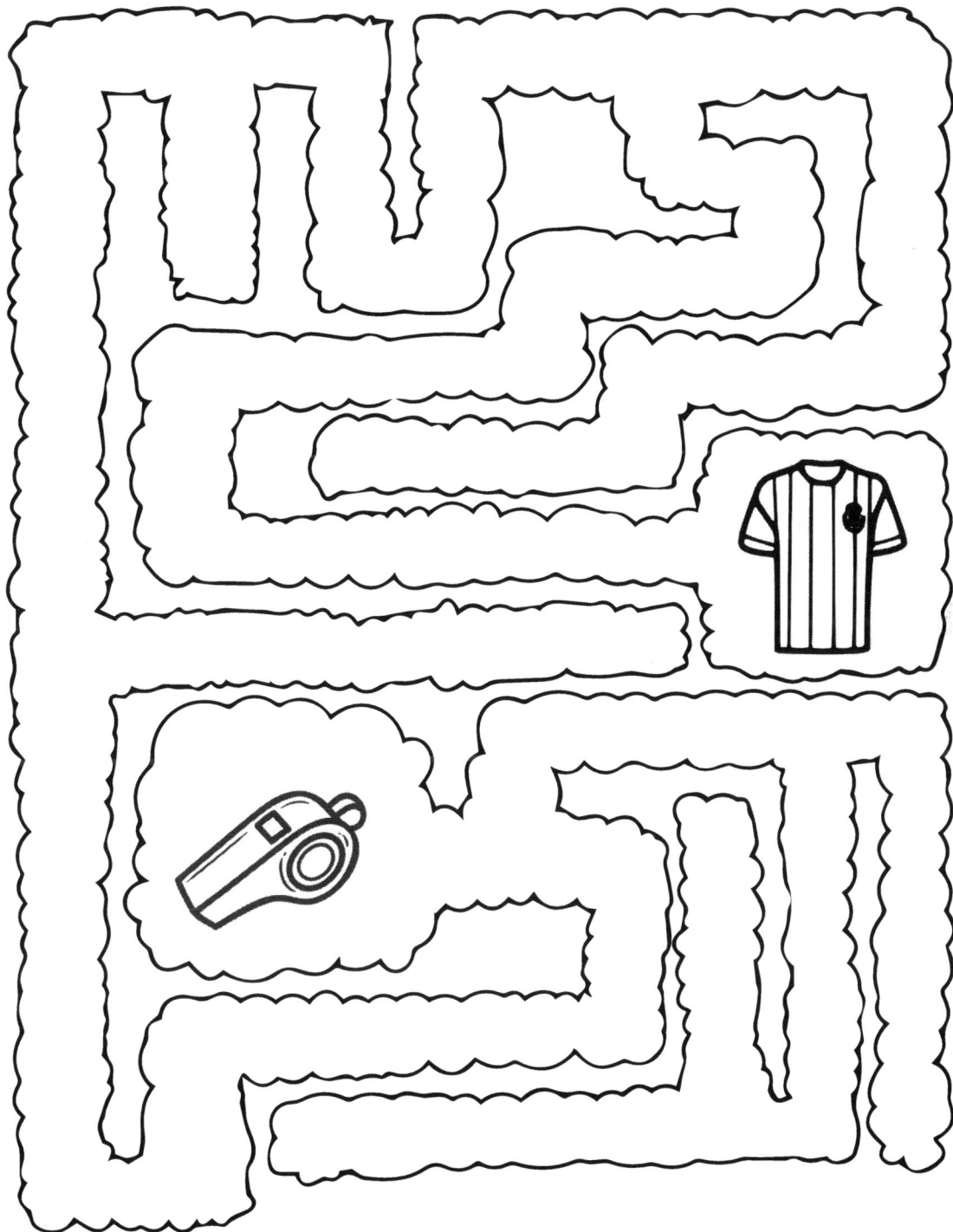

FOOTBALL WORDSEARCH #8

Get ready to score! Find all the football words hidden in the puzzle. Keep your eyes sharp and kick off the search!

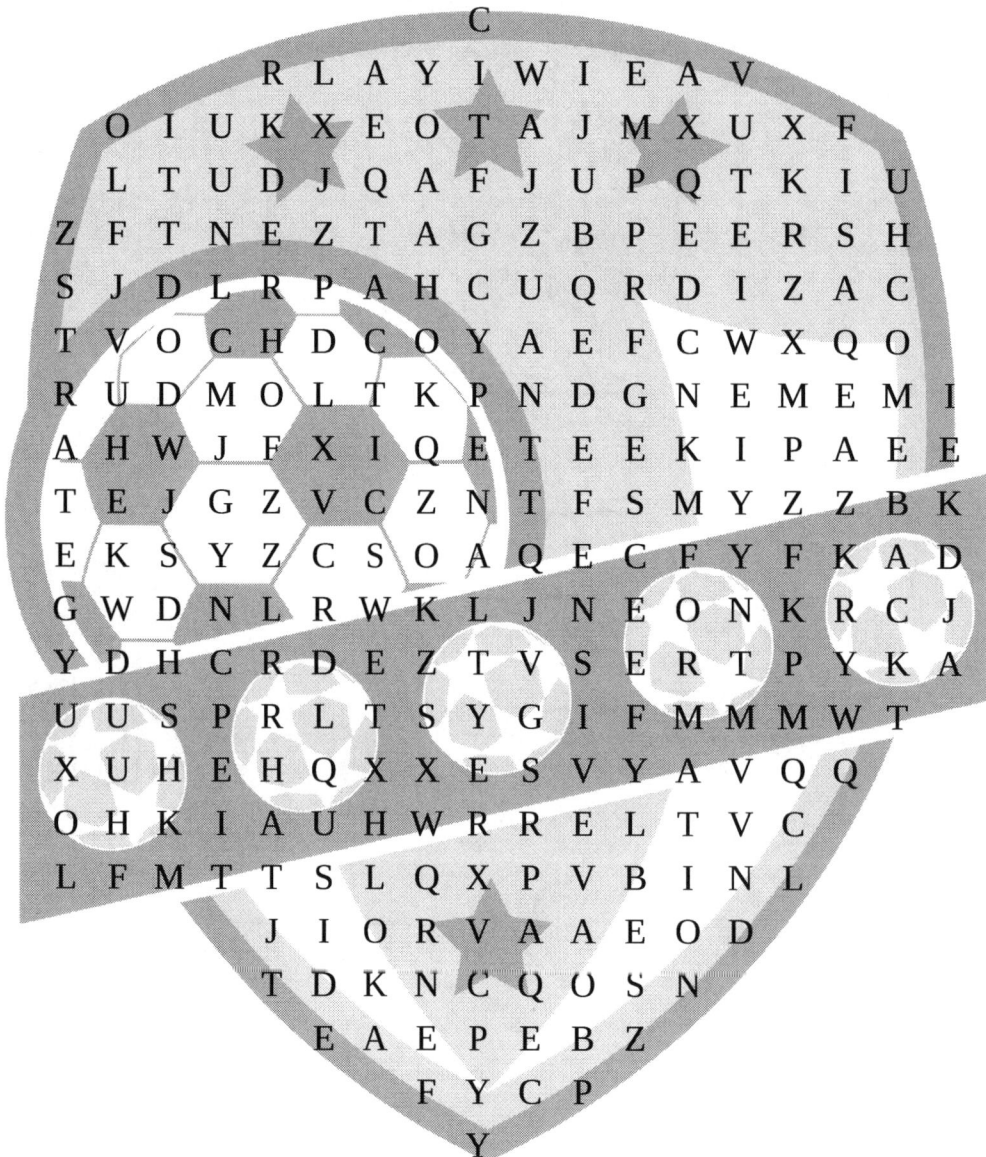

```
              C
      R L A Y I W I E A V
    O I U K X E O T A J M X U X F
    L T U D J Q A F J U P Q T K I U
  Z F T N E Z T A G Z B P E E R S H
  S J D L R P A H C U Q R D I Z A C
  T V O C H D C O Y A E F C W X Q O
  R U D M O L T K P N D G N E M E M I
  A H W J F X I Q E T E E K I P A E E
  T E J G Z V C Z N T F S M Y Z Z B K
  E K S Y Z C S O A Q E C F Y F K A D
  G W D N L R W K L J N E O N K R C J
  Y D H C R D E Z T V S E R T P Y K A
  U U S P R L T S Y G I F M M M W T
  X U H E H Q X X E S V Y A V Q Q
  O H K I A U H W R R E L T V C
  L F M T T S L Q X P V B I N L
        J I O R V A A E O D
        T D K N C Q O S N
        E A E P E B Z
          F Y C P
            Y
```

ACADEMY	COMEBACK	DEFENSIVE
EXTRA	FORMATION	LEAGUE
PENALTY	RESERVE	SEASON
STRATEGY	TACTICS	

FOOTBALL FACTS

Most Trophies Won by a Manager:

Sir Alex Ferguson also holds the record for the most trophies won by a manager, with 49 trophies across his managerial career, including league titles, domestic cups, and European trophies.

Most Successful Manager in European Football:

Carlo Ancelotti has won the UEFA Champions League five times, the most by any manager, with AC Milan (2003, 2007) and Real Madrid (2014, 2022, 2024).

KICKOFF CRYPTOGRAM CHALLENGE! #7

Use the clues in the legend to match letters and reveal the secret football phrase!

A	B	C	D	E	F	G	H	I	J	K	L	M
📋	⚽	👟	🚩	👕	GOAL	🧣	🩳	🧦	🔺	FC	🏳️	🏟️

N	O	P	Q	R	S	T	U	V	W	X	Y	Z
🏁	🧰	🥅	👟	🥅	🟥	⏱️	👟	📣	IN/OUT	🧤	7:0	🔔

1.

[shorts][jersey][clipboard][corner flag] [sock][stopwatch] [stopwatch][first aid] [stopwatch][shorts][jersey]

[scarf][first aid][clipboard][flag] !

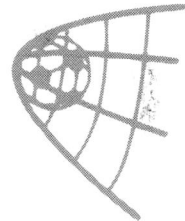

Hint: Use your head to score!

2.

[FC][sock][boot][FC] [sock][stopwatch] [stopwatch][first aid]

[in/out][sock][checkered flag] [sock][stopwatch] !

Hint: Take the shot that could win the game!

THE FOOTBALL MAZE RUN #9

Quick! Help the lad score a goal before the timer runs out!

Brilliant! You beat the clock and scored — top skills!

DESIGN YOUR OWN FOOTBALL

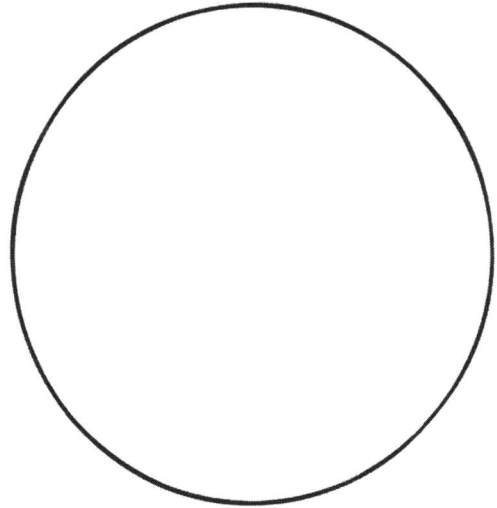

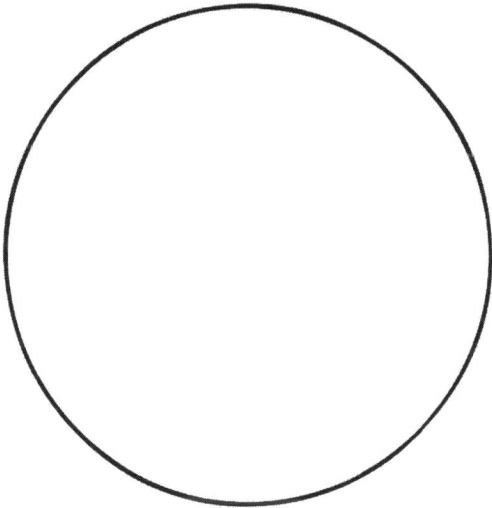

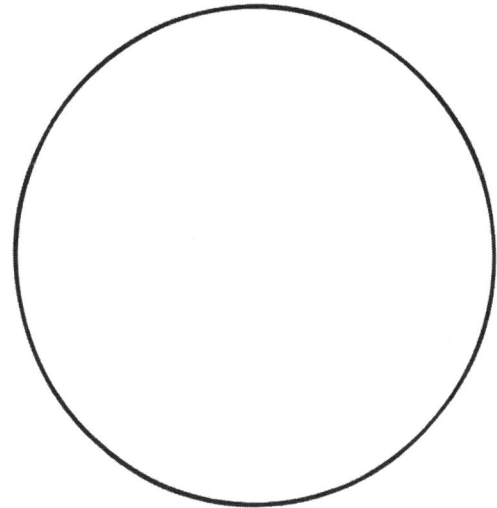

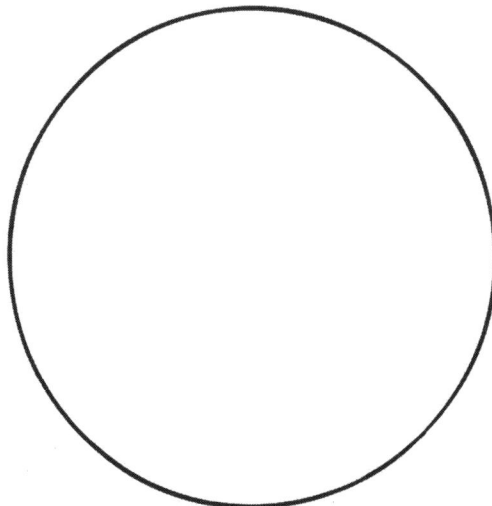

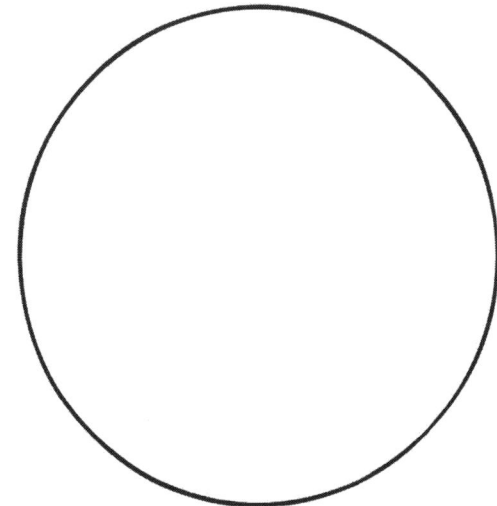

FOOTBALL WORDSEARCH #9

Get ready to score! Find all the football words hidden in the puzzle. Keep your eyes sharp and kick off the search!

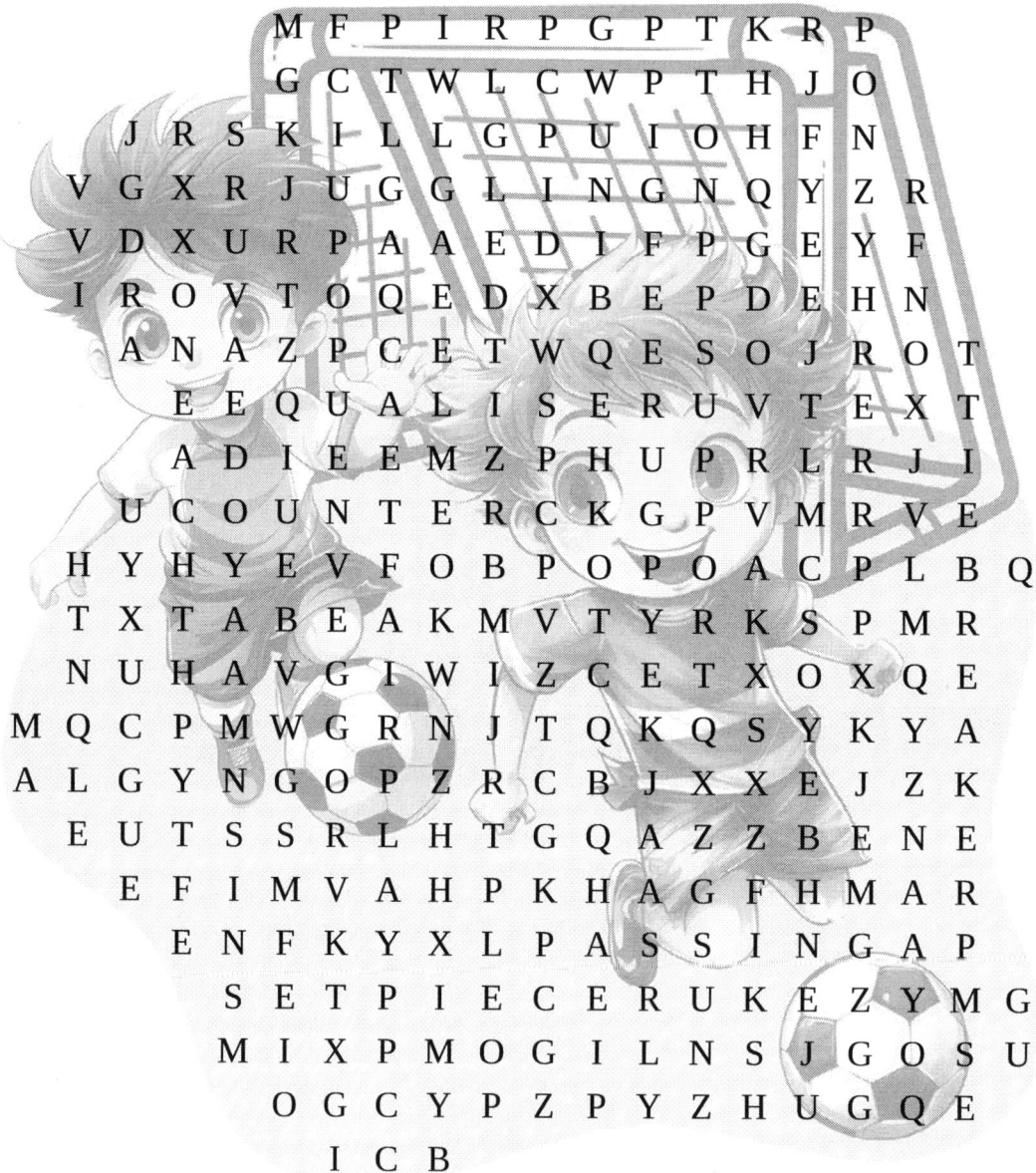

```
M F P I R P G P T K R P
G C T W L C W P T H J O
J R S K I L L G P U I O H F N
V G X R J U G G L I N G N Q Y Z R
V D X U R P A A E D I F P G E Y F
I R O V T O Q E D X B E P D E H N
A N A Z P C E T W Q E S O J R O T
E E Q U A L I S E R U V T E X T
A D I E E M Z P H U P R L R J I
U C O U N T E R C K G P V M R V E
H Y H Y E V F O B P O P O A C P L B Q
T X T A B E A K M V T Y R K S P M R
N U H A V G I W I Z C E T X O X Q E
M Q C P M W G R N J T Q K Q S Y K Y A
A L G Y N G O P Z R C B J X X E J Z K
E U T S S R L H T G Q A Z Z B E N E
E F I M V A H P K H A G F H M A R
E N F K Y X L P A S S I N G A P
S E T P I E C E R U K E Z Y M G
M I X P M O G I L N S J G O S U
O G C Y P Z P Y Z H U G Q E
I C B
```

COUNTER	EQUALISER	FAIRPLAY
JUGGLING	KITBAG	PASSING
SETPIECE	SKILL	SUPPORT
TIEBREAKER	WINGER	

DESIGN YOUR OWN TEAM BADGE

Create your own badge

KICKOFF CRYPTOGRAM CHALLENGE! #8

Use the clues in the legend to match letters and reveal the secret football phrase!

A	B	C	D	E	F	G	H	I	J	K	L	M

N	O	P	Q	R	S	T	U	V	W	X	Y	Z

1. DEFEND LIKE A LION!

Hint: Protect your goal with bravery!

2. PLAY WITH HEART AND HUSTLE!

Hint: Show lots of energy and determination!

WORD UNSCRAMBLE #4

Hint - Premier League Football Teams 2025/2026

VENROET

_ _ _ _ _ _ _

HAMFUL

_ _ _ _ _ _

MANTOETTH

_ _ _ _ _ _ _ _ _

SALECHE

_ _ _ _ _ _ _

WETSEANCL

_ _ _ _ _ _ _ _ _

YOUR GK FOOTBALL CARD

Overall Rating

Position

GK

Nationality

Your Image

Name

Diving   ___ **DIV**   ___ **REF**   Reflexes

Handling   ___ **HAN**   ___ **SPD**   Speed

Kicking   ___ **KIC**   ___ **POS**   Positioning

Autograph

Example

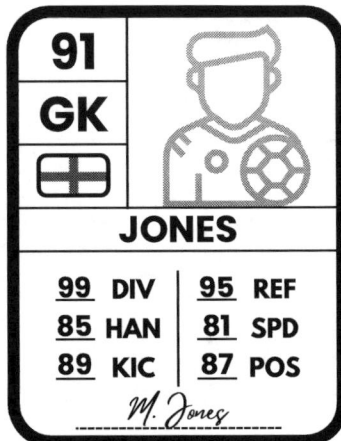

91	
GK	
🏴	
JONES	

99 DIV	95 REF
85 HAN	81 SPD
89 KIC	87 POS

M. Jones

THE FOOTBALL MAZE RUN #10

The coach forgot his playbook! Help the player find it before the big match!

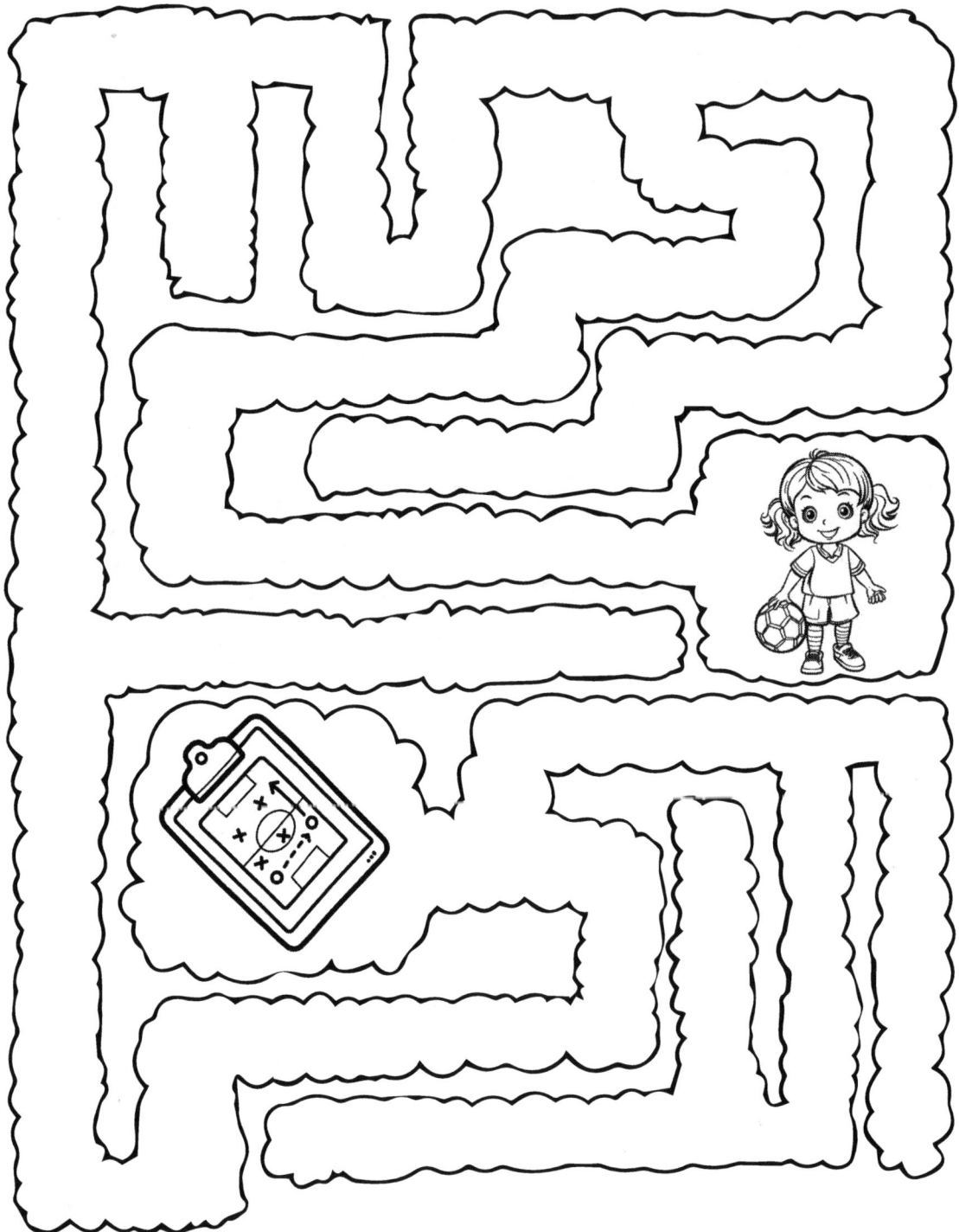

CAN YOU PREDICT THE FUTURE?

Which team do you think will win the Premier League in the 2025/2026 season?

....

Which three teams will be relegated to the Championship at the end of the season?

....

Who will be the top goal scorer in the Premier League this season?

....

Which club will win the UEFA Champions League in the 2025/2026 season?

....

Who do you think will win the Ballon d'Or in 2026?

....

KICKOFF CRYPTOGRAM CHALLENGE! #9

Use the clues in the legend to match letters and reveal the secret football phrase!

A	B	C	D	E	F	G	H	I	J	K	L	M
N	O	P	Q	R	S	T	U	V	W	X	Y	Z

1.

TRAIN HARD,

PLAY HARDER!

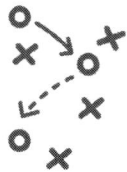

Hint: Practise loads so you're ready for the game!

2.

CHASE THE BALL,

CHASE THE DREAM

Hint: Follow your passion for football!

FOOTBALL FACTS

First Black Player to Play for England:

Viv Anderson was the first Black footballer to represent England at the senior international level, making his debut in 1978.

First Asian Team to Reach World Cup Semi-Finals:

South Korea became the first Asian team to reach the World Cup semi-finals in 2002.

FOOTBALL WORDSEARCH #10

Get ready to score! Find all the football words hidden in the puzzle. Keep your eyes sharp and kick off the search!

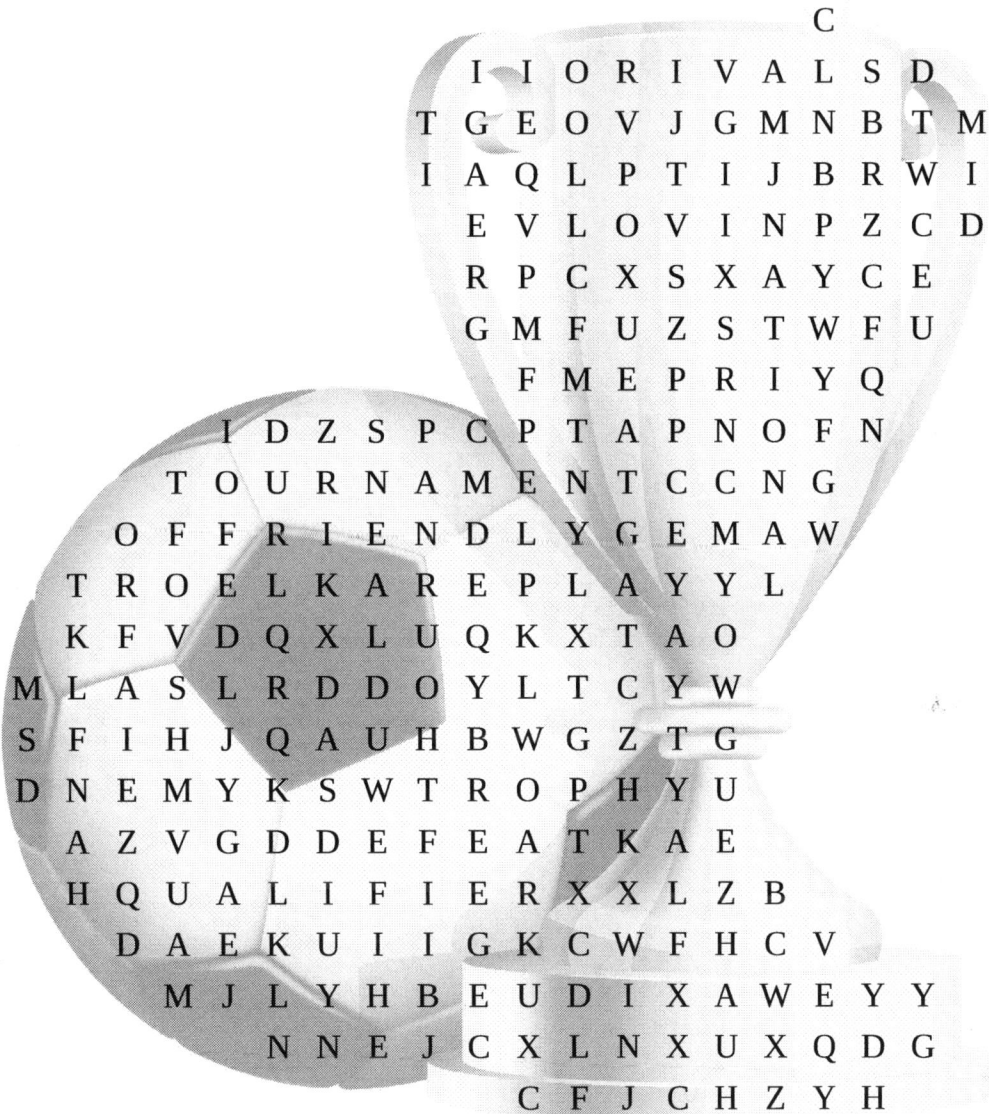

```
                              C
              I I O R I V A L S D
              T G E O V J G M N B T M
              I A Q L P T I J B R W I
              E V L O V I N P Z C D
              R P C X S X A Y C E
              G M F U Z S T W F U
              F M E P R I Y Q
          I D Z S P C P T A P N O F N
        T O U R N A M E N T C C N G
        O F F R I E N D L Y G E M A W
      T R O E L K A R E P L A Y Y L
      K F V D Q X L U Q K X T A O
    M L A S L R D D O Y L T C Y W
    S F I H J Q A U H B W G Z T G
    D N E M Y K S W T R O P H Y U
    A Z V G D D E F E A T K A E
    H Q U A L I F I E R X X L Z B
      D A E K U I I G K C W F H C V
      M J L Y H B E U D I X A W E Y Y
        N N E J C X L N X U X Q D G
              C F J C H Z Y H
```

CUP	DEFEAT	DRAW
FRIENDLY	LOSS	NATIONAL
QUALIFIER	REPLAY	RIVALS
TOURNAMENT	TROPHY	WIN

THE FOOTBALL MAZE RUN #11

Congratulations on making the team! Guide him through the maze to pick up his new jersey!

BRILLIANT!

YOU'RE ON YOUR WAY TO BEING A FOOTBALL STAR!

YOUR FOOTBALL CARD

Overall
Rating

Position

Nationality

Your
Image

Name

Pace
Shooting
Passing

___ **PAC**   ___ **SKL**
___ **SHO**   ___ **DEF**
___ **PAS**   ___ **PHY**

Skill
Defending
Physicality

Autograph

Example

91
ST

JONES

99 PAC   **95** SKL
85 SHO   **81** DEF
89 PAS   **87** PHY

M. Jones

KICKOFF CRYPTOGRAM CHALLENGE! #10

Use the clues in the legend to match letters and reveal the secret football phrase!

A	B	C	D	E	F	G	H	I	J	K	L	M
⏱	📋	GOAL	⇄	👟	👞	⚽	🏟	🥅	🚩	🚩	🩳	7:0

N	O	P	Q	R	S	T	U	V	W	X	Y	Z
📣	🟨	🔺	FC	👕	🧣	🧤	🧰	🧦	⚽	📣	🥅	🏁

1. SHOOT FOR THE STARS !

Hint: Aim high and go for the win!

2. AIM HIGH , SCORE BIG !

Hint: Set your sights on the top!

FOOTBALL FACTS

First All-Female Refereeing Team in a Men's English Football League Game:

In 2023, an EFL League Two match between Harrogate Town and Sutton United was officiated by an all-female refereeing team for the first time.

First Woman to Manage an English Men's Team:

Hannah Dingley became the first female manager of a men's professional football club in England, taking charge of Forest Green Rovers in 2023.

PICK YOUR PERFECT TEAM

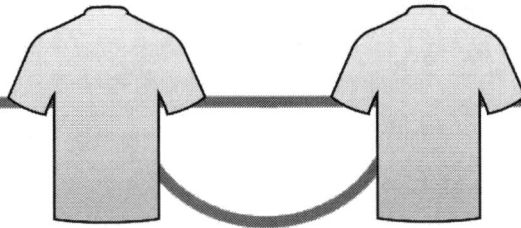

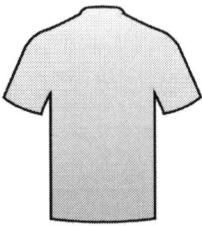

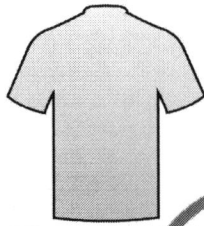

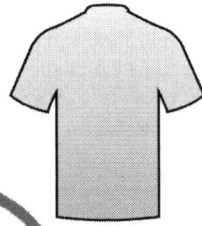

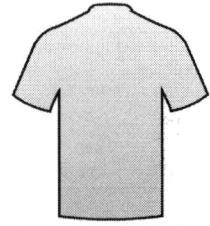

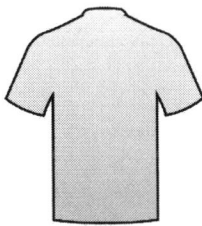

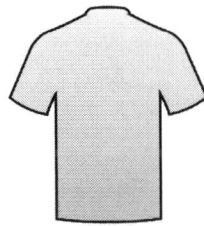

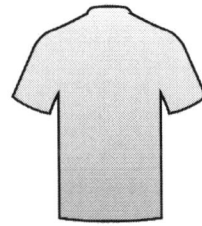

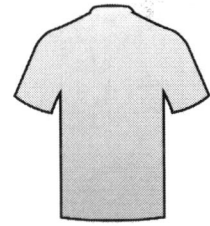

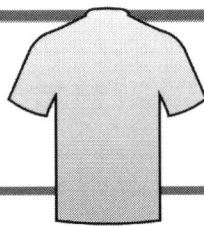

THE FOOTBALL MAZE RUN #12

Help the lad make his way through the maze to grab his match ticket!

DESIGN YOUR OWN FOOTBALL KIT

FOOTBALL FACTS

The Oldest Football Club:

Sheffield FC in England, founded in 1857, is the world's oldest football club and is still active today!

Ouch, I've got a headache!:

In the early days of football, balls were made from leather and became very heavy when wet, making heading the ball dangerous.

DESIGN YOUR OWN FOOTBALL KIT

FOOTBALL FACTS

Most Goals in a Premier League Season:

Erling Haaland holds the record for the most goals scored in a single Premier League season, netting 36 goals in the 2022-23 campaign.

Goalkeeper with Most Career Goals:

Brazilian goalkeeper Rogério Ceni scored over 131 goals during his career, mostly from free kicks and penalties.

DESIGN YOUR OWN FOOTBALL KIT

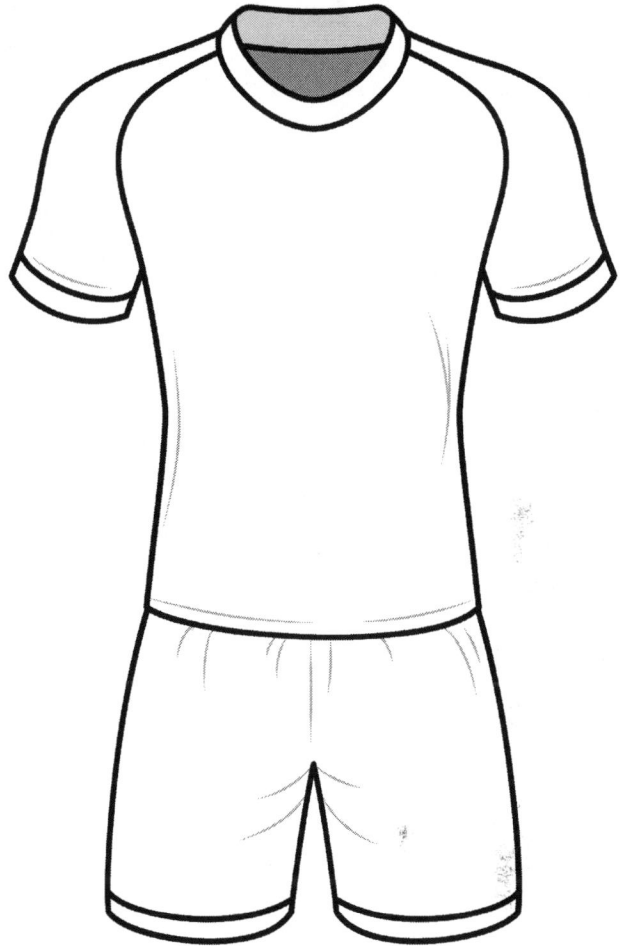

FOOTBALL FACTS

Most Champions League Titles:

Real Madrid has won the UEFA Champions League 15 times, the most of any club. (As of 2024)

The World Cup Trophy Kidnapping:

In 1966, before the World Cup in England, the Jules Rimet Trophy was stolen from an exhibition. A week later, it was found by a dog named Pickles, who became a national hero.

DESIGN YOUR OWN FOOTBALL KIT

FOOTBALL FACTS

First Footballer Knighted While Playing:

Sir Stanley Matthews is the only footballer to have been knighted while still actively playing football. He was knighted in 1965, just before retiring at the age of 50.

Astronaut Neil Armstrong, the first man on the moon, reportedly said he wished he had brought a football to kick around during his lunar expedition in 1969, as part of a joke on the popularity of the sport worldwide.

DESIGN YOUR OWN FOOTBALL KIT

FOOTBALL FACTS

World Cup Origins:

The first FIFA World Cup was held in 1930 in Uruguay. The hosts also won the tournament.

UEFA Women's Champions League:

Lyon is the most successful club in UEFA Women's Champions League history, having won the tournament 8 times (as of 2024).

DESIGN YOUR OWN GOALKEEPER KIT

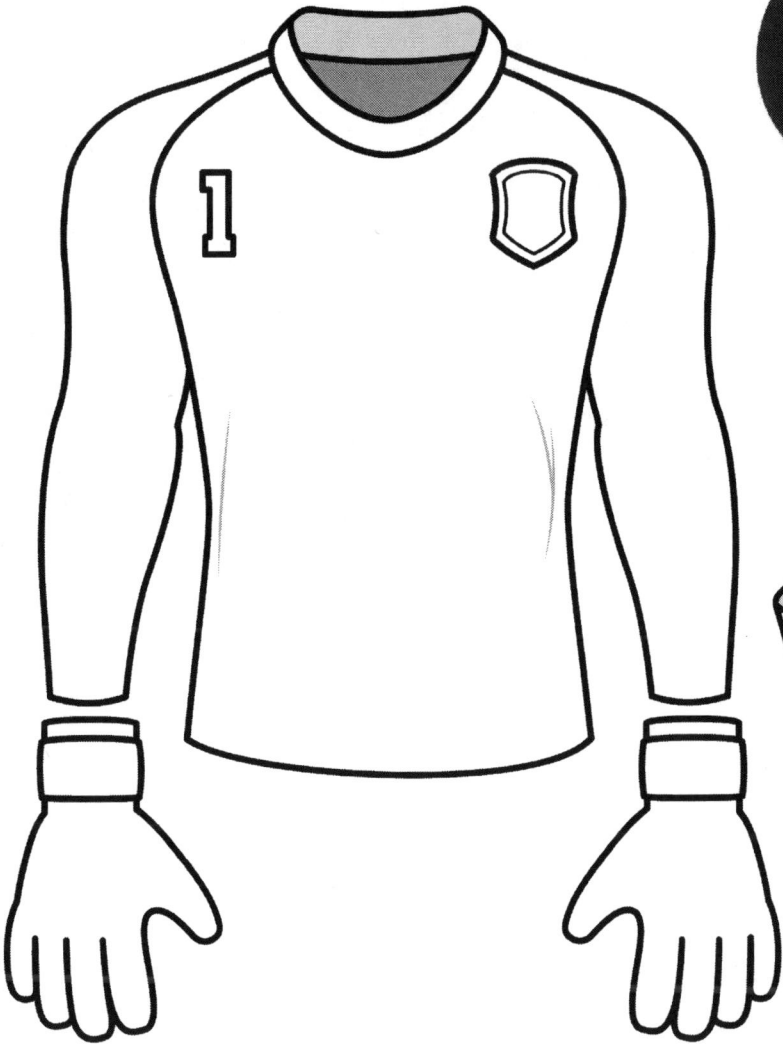

FOOTBALL

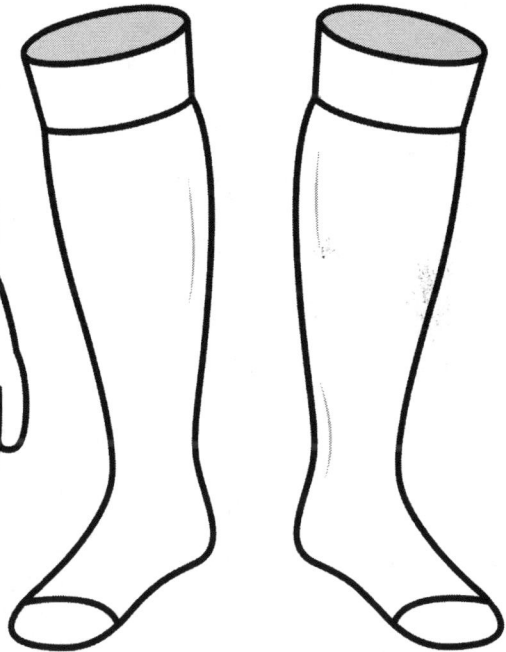

FOOTBALL FACTS

Oldest Football Tournament:

The FA Cup, first held in 1871, is the oldest football competition in the world.

Ballon d'Or Wins:

Lionel Messi holds the record for the most Ballon d'Or awards, with 7 wins (as of 2024).

DESIGN YOUR OWN BOOTS

FOOTBALL FACTS

Longest Goal:

The longest goal ever scored was by Tom King, a goalkeeper for Newport County, in January 2021. The goal was 96.01 meters (105 yards).

Longest Unbeaten Run in English Football:

Arsenal went 49 matches unbeaten between May 2003 and October 2004, earning the nickname "The Invincibles" after their unbeaten 2003-04 season.

DESIGN YOUR OWN BOOTS

FOOTBALL FACTS

Most Hat-Tricks in Football:

Cristiano Ronaldo holds the record for the most hat-tricks in men's football, having scored 63 hat-tricks in official matches (as of 2024). This includes hat-tricks for both club and country, making him one of the most prolific goal scorers in the sport's history.

Longest-Serving Manager:

Sir Alex Ferguson managed Manchester United for 27 years, from 1986 to 2013, becoming the longest-serving manager in Premier League history.

HOW TO PLAY FOOTBALL SUDOKU: ASSIGN, WRITE, AND WIN!

Welcome, young puzzle masters! In Football Sudoku, your goal is to fill the grid by assigning a unique number to each football-themed image. With a bit of strategy, creativity, and patience, you'll score big! Ready to play? Let's get started!

HOW THE GAME WORKS:

Assign a number or to each image.

- In the dashed box to the side of the puzzle, write the number that you've chosen for each image.
  - Example: ⚽ = 1, 🏟️ = 2, 🎺📣 3, 🚩👟⚽

Use your assignments to fill the empty spaces.

- Write the matching number or letter in each blank cell, making sure you follow the Sudoku rules below.

THREE GENERAL RULES OF SUDOKU:

1. Each row must contain every symbol exactly once.
   - No duplicates allowed!

2. Each column must contain every symbol exactly once.
   - Double-check each column for the same image.

3. Each smaller box must contain every symbol exactly once.

- In a 4x4 grid, that means each 2x2 box should have one of each soccer-themed image.

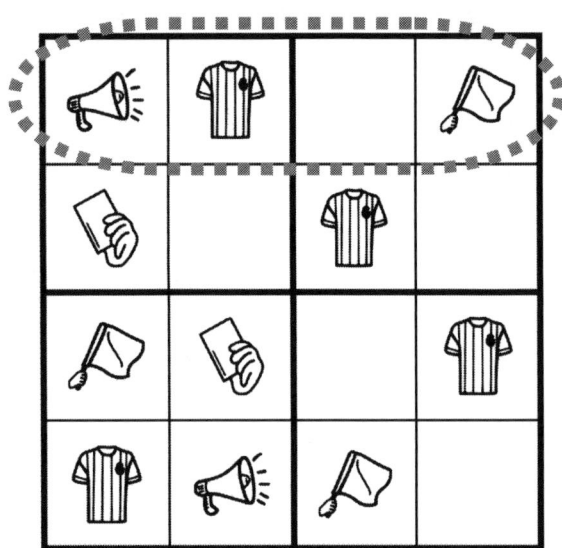

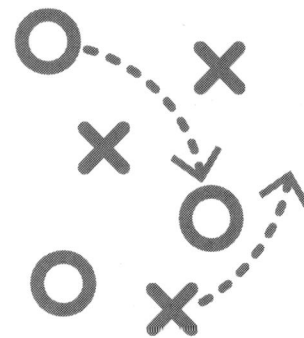

GOAL!!!

HELPFUL HINTS:

- Start with what you know! Look for rows, columns, or boxes that already have some clues filled in.

- Work section by section. Fill in the easiest areas first—this will help you solve the tougher spots.

- Stay organized! Use a pencil to make changes easily if you spot a mistake.

GOAL-TIME SUDOKU: FINISH STRONG AND CELEBRATE!

Example of Play:

- Step 1: Assign numbers:

  ⚽ (Ball) = 1, 🏀(Whistle) = 2, 👕(Jersey) = 3, 🚩🏳(Flag) = 4

- Step 2: Now, fill the grid with your chosen numbers:

  If the top-left corner has a whistle 🏀 write 2 in that box. If the first row already has a flag 🏳 make sure you don't repeat it!

Stay focused, think carefully, and don't give up! You're just a few moves away from scoring a Sudoku goal!

FOOTBALL SUDOKU: LEARN THE MOVES TO WIN!

① *Warm-Up Drills: Practice Your Puzzle Skills!*

②

You're on the attack! Every move gets you closer to victory—keep going!

GAME PLAN IN ACTION: LEARN THE MOVES TO WIN!

③

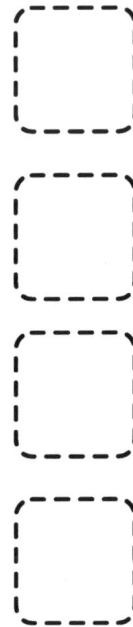

④

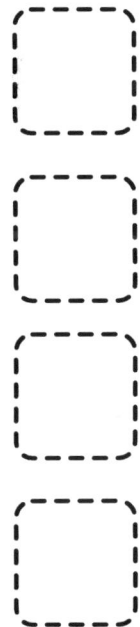

Don't stop now! Your next brilliant move could be the game-changer!

GAME PLAN IN ACTION: LEARN THE MOVES TO WIN!

⑤

⑥

Kick it into high gear! You're solving puzzles like a pro!

GAME PLAN IN ACTION: LEARN THE MOVES TO WIN!

⑦

⑧

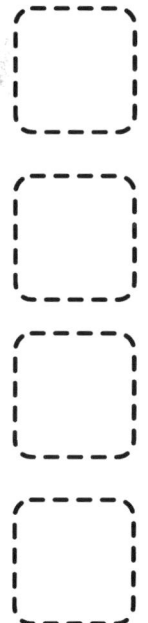

Stay sharp, superstar! Every box filled is a step toward the goal!

GAME PLAN IN ACTION: LEARN THE MOVES TO WIN!

⑨

⑩

Great teamwork between your brain and pencil! You're almost there!

SOLUTION SECTION

Congratulations on completing this book!

I hope it has brought you hours of fun and entertainment.

Don't want the fun to stop?

Grab **20 more bonus activities** for **FREE** as an extra thank-you!

Just scan the QR code

Or visit - " bit.ly/FOOTYBONUS2 "
(Caps sensitive)

Can I ask for a tiny favour please?

Despite the saying, people **do** judge a book by its cover and its reviews.

If this book was enjoyed, it would mean the world to me if you could leave a review on Amazon.

Your feedback helps me to continue creating books that inspire kids to learn, and grow.

As a solo publisher, your support & reviews truly make a difference in my journey.

Thank you so much!

Casey

How to Leave the review:

Scan this QR code with your phone camera. 👈

Or...

Go to **Amazon > Your Orders**, find our book, and click **"Write a Product Review."**
Even a simple rating helps more than you could imagine.

GAME PLAN IN ACTION: SOLUTIONS

Puzzle 1

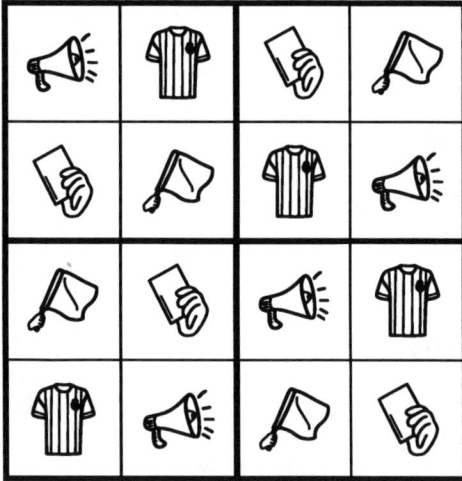

Puzzle 2

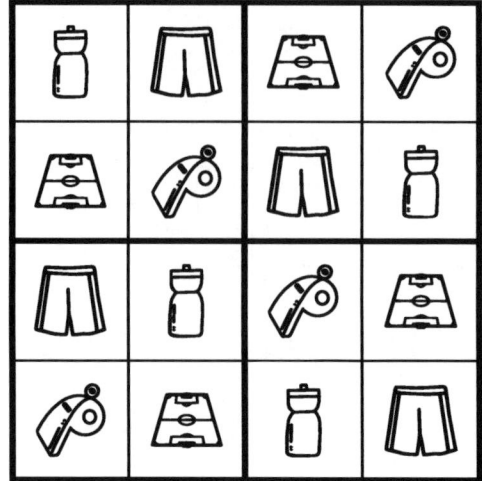

Puzzle 3

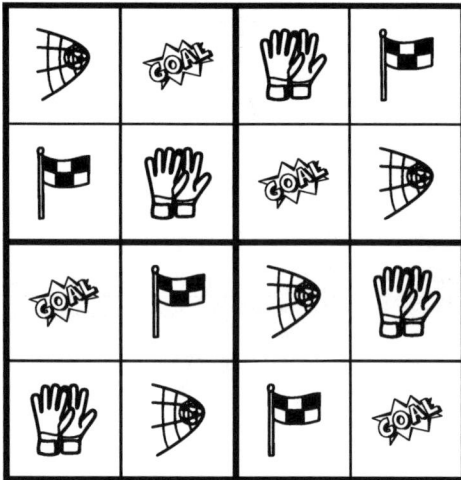

Puzzle 4

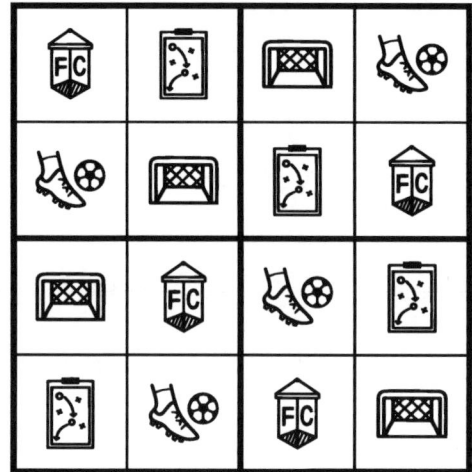

Puzzle 5

Puzzle 6

GAME PLAN IN ACTION: SOLUTIONS

Puzzle 7

Puzzle 8

Puzzle 9

Puzzle 10

GOAL SCORED! YOU TACKLED THESE PUZZLES LIKE A PRO – WELL DONE!

THE FOOTBALL MAZE RUN SOLUTIONS!

Maze 1, The Football Maze Run!

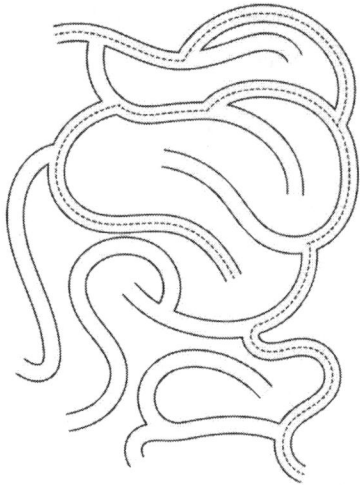

Maze 2, The Football Maze Run!

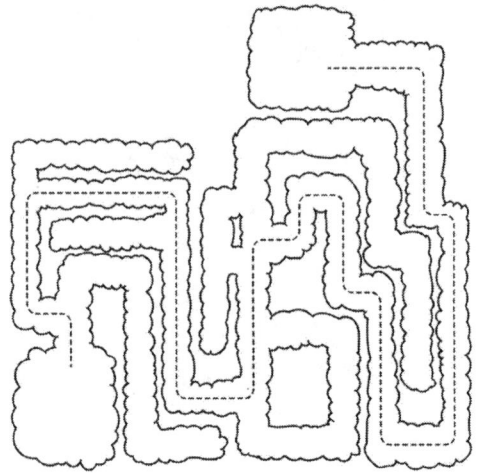

Maze 3, The Football Maze Run!

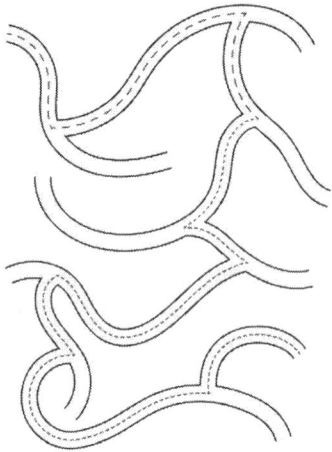

Maze 4, The Football Maze Run!

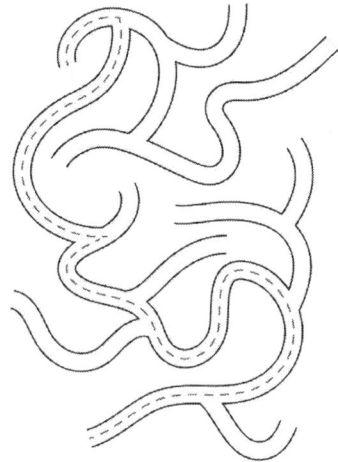

Maze 5, The Football Maze Run!

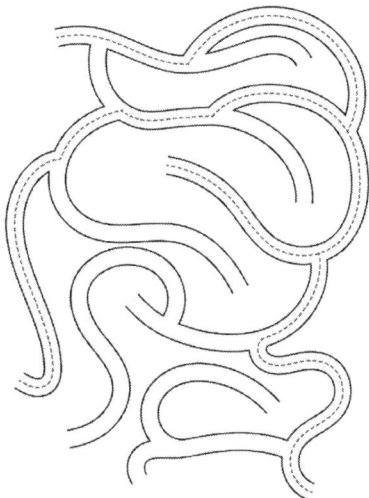

Maze 6, The Football Maze Run!

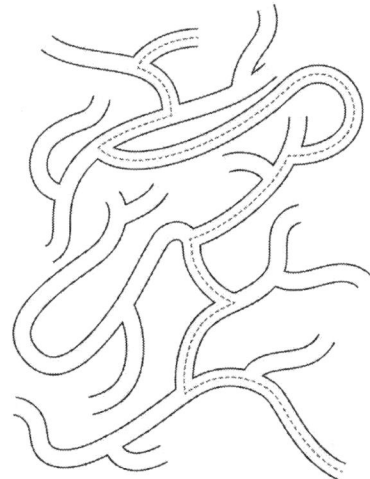

THE FOOTBALL MAZE RUN SOLUTIONS!

Maze 7, The Football Maze Run!

Maze 8, The Football Maze Run!

Maze 9, The Football Maze Run!

Maze 10, The Football Maze Run!

Maze 11, The Football Maze Run!

Maze 12, The Football Maze Run!

FOOTBALL WORDSEARCH SOLUTIONS

Puzzle 1, Football Wordsearch

```
                    I A
              X F S M A Y G B
              KICK L Q O O I F Z I
              Y A N U U G O T D F O V E O
        U B I O J Y T K R K G A V S E R
        B K W Q W V K B Q R Q G A C A X
        D O I M K D H K N W X T O M O B X
        Z I V U F G O X P RUN A U R T P X
        K M B B E A Q S Y M C V L B E G N H
        G W Y J C H Z H K G B G W C Q G J
        V O Z D V K T S I B A W A P U N Z W
        P M G T W U Q F C Q L V T L L U F N
        X O S E A D K J K M L F E A F J A Q
        M I R P R R E T O W J G S Y E J N D
        S G X M R I B S F H P O C O K H Z
        G J F U P B A F V E K P F P H F K
        Z R P R B V U J B H N A F U C
              Q Q L U E J L M W S T D
              E I E B S Q T S
                    P Q
```

Puzzle 2, Football Wordsearch

```
                    C G E
              R BOOTS
              TEAMMATE
              B S H W K N B R
        V M D E X   G I R Y I L W M
        TEAMWORK Z H Q S Q T
        T D N M G T       W N U Z K
        H X E Q C             N
        R T C                 D N T
        R K Q I             R U K X F
    E Q P W Z T           A P E W M
        Y Q Z N I   F M D A D G C
        B F Q YOUTH D M D D P M
        H X GOALKEEPER I C O A
        CLUB E Q M K H N O W Z T C
        H I L M Y D L M Z B O C H P
        PRACTICE E X Z H C
              U T H JERSEY A H
                    L R H Y T X
```

Puzzle 3, Football Wordsearch

```
    Y V L N Z J SIDELINE J T S M
    J U Z P F T N N W X P W J M A T S I
    B G Y M F Y K X R I V C L P M D U C
    G M L V I K J U U S I D V M O P W K
    P S T A T W Z Q G N D K A A D X I O
    E O F G N U A DIVE I Z Y B K C A
    H J O D E M L V T P B T R E P E N O
    U Q O E S D P T M T X C Z CROSS
    L S T F S M H C L H X M X G Y A C T
    D J B E F A R SPRINT Z C S M O
    A J A N I T N R L U C N N F U P G O
    W O E L D B C J STRIKER I L R Q R
    U D L E H T M V F L V I G G Z A V
    N F R E M Y D X U Y R M Q Q F O
        X Y D H A D U O J K D R D
              F P K Y V Z
```

Puzzle 4, Football Wordsearch

```
                    F R
              Y P K Y H S B W L D
              T G N F N L E F K K
        N L F P R J Q N N L Q G F G N R J C J N
        R R G S D C NET Y S W I S V E L E D X
        MANAGER FANS V T A FOUL F C
        J POINTS T T O T L A B B A S Y U A
        Z X W R M G U V Z P H G C Q P L H Z L S
        O D L L O G X L M C W Z K M V M I Q L T
        F K R R J O Y D H H Z T L F E O N M T T
        L H C G D Z O F C M G C E L M S P I I I
        M G X STANDS Q R C N F D X A A M R
        D S W Y F Y G S T D A O L X N V D X E T
        A R F Q D V O P V G S H F B H H M W Z X
        J O G K O M Z T S X S U O D T I U M X H
        O N Z Z Q U I I J T O X T G W M O T X P
```

Puzzle 5, Football Wordsearch

```
                    E E O Y S
        T Z SHOT L Z U H P H K
        I A S O X D E E E A I T D
        M S F T C T Q U D L R A A
        H K TURF T E F I K P
        D I D D U J S H R T T S B
        Y E E W I R W R B I Q Z O
        S L F G L C X O Y M M E Y
        B D E F Y Q W E W T E H J D
    Y J Q E I N T G Y U F F CORNER
    T N M S N C L J R B G J P O L M W C
            G E T WHISTLE I
              U V M T B M R R W
```

Puzzle 6, Football Wordsearch

```
                    B O J H
                  P Z J K U T S
                U Y N N V R C X X G
                B U E J B O W P J Q H
                Q MATCHDAY U X O L
                F SHOTSTOPPER N
            R   Y M Y D A M REFEREE
        S T T N J GOALPOST E Y A T
        E V A E C V G I G B J U F M I A I R
        F POSSESSION FINAL I A
        E M O O K V D D N W X W T N D G I
        L R B P O O K B U C N E J S R L O N
        T W T L Y Y A T A Z B R P R G O I N
        K Y U B U S U Q U A W Q M V L L G
        G H O J P R Y W I G T V E T C
        N V SQUAD U J H S C
              O Z C PLAYER
              S P Y J T G
                    Y P
                    H
```

FOOTBALL WORDSEARCH SOLUTIONS

Puzzle 7, Football Wordsearch

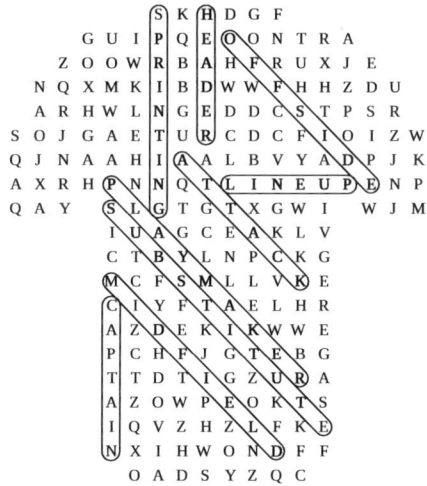

```
              S K H D G F
      G U I P Q E O O N T R A
    Z O O W R B A H F R U X J E
  N Q X M K I B D W W F H H Z D U
  A R H W L N G E D D C S T P S R
  S O J G A E T U R C D C F I O I Z W
  Q J N A A H I A A L B V Y A D P J K
  A X R H P N N Q T L I N E U P E N P
  Q A Y   S L G T G T X G W I   W J M
            I U A G C E A K L V
            C T B Y L N P C K G
            M C F S M L L V K E
            C I Y F T A E L H R
            A Z D E K I K W W E
            P C H F J G T E B G
            T T D T I G Z U R A
            A A Z O W P E O K T S
            I Q V Z H Z L F K E
            N X I H W O N D F F
              O A D S Y Z Q C
```

Puzzle 8, Football Wordsearch

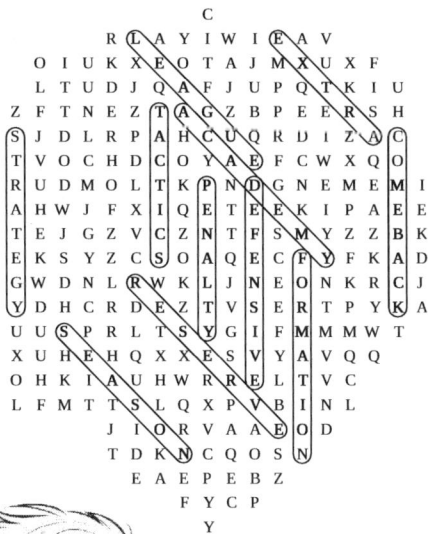

```
                    C
        R L A Y I W I E A V
    O I U K X E O T A J M X U X F
    L T U D J Q A F J U P Q T K I U
  Z F T N E Z T A G Z B P E E R S H
  S J D L R P A H C U Q R D I Z A C
  T V O C H D C O Y A E F C W X Q O
  R U D M O L T K P N D G N E M E M I
  A H W J F X I Q E T E E K I P A E E
  T E J G Z V C Z N T F S M Y Z Z B K
  E K S Y Z C S O A Q E C F Y F K A D
  G W D N L R W K L J N E O N K R C J
  Y D H C R D E Z T S Y E R T P Y K A
  U U S P R L T S Y G I F M M M W T
  X U H E H Q X X E S V Y A V Q Q
  O H K I A U H W R R E L T V C
  L F M T T S L Q X P V B I N L
        J I O R V A A E O D
        T D K N C Q O S
          E A E P E B Z
            F Y C P
              Y
```

Puzzle 9, Football Wordsearch

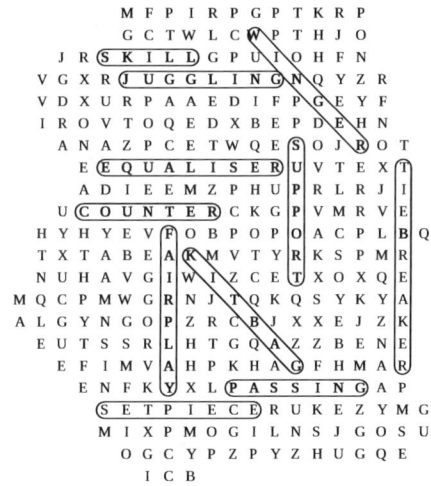

```
          M F P I R P G P T K R P
          G C T W L C W P T H J O
        J R S K I L L G P U O H F N
      V G X R J U G G L I N G N Q Y Z R
      V D X U R P A A E D I F P G E Y F
      I R O V T O Q E D X B E P D E H N
      A N A Z P C E T W Q E S O J R O T
      E E Q U A L I S E R U V T E X I
      A D I E E M Z P H U P R L R J I
      U C O U N T E R C K G P V M R V E
    H Y H Y E V F O B P O P O A C P L B Q
    T X T A B E A K M V T Y R K S P M R
    N U H A V G I W I Z C E T X O X Q E
    M Q C P M W G R N J T Q K Q S Y K Y A
    A L G Y N G O P Z R C B J X X E J Z K
    E U T S S R L H T G Q A Z Z B E N E
    E F I M V A H P K H A G F H M A R
    E N F K Y X L P A S S I N G A P
      S E T P I E C E R U K E Z Y M G
        M I X P M O G I L N S J G O S U
        O G C Y P Z P Y Z H U G Q E
          I C B
```

Puzzle 10, Football Wordsearch

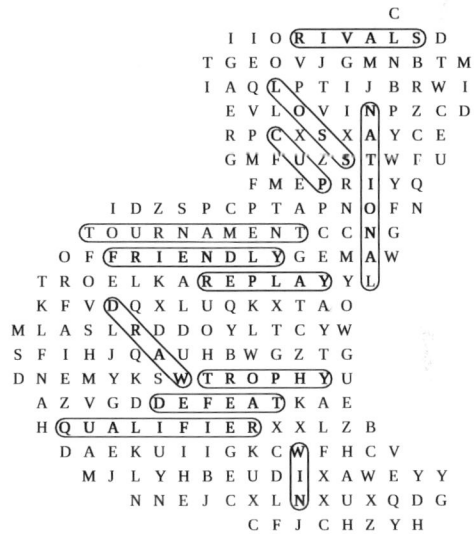

```
                    C
      I I O R I V A L S D
    T G E O V J G M N B T M
    I A Q L P T I J B R W I
    E V L O V I N P Z C D
    R P C X S X A Y C E
    G M F U Z S T W F U
      F M E P R I Y Q
    I D Z S P C P T A P N O F N
  T O U R N A M E N T C C N G
    O F F R I E N D L Y G E M A W
  T R O E L K A R E P L A Y Y L
  K F V D Q X L U Q K X T A O
  M L A S L R D D O Y L T C Y W
  S F I H J Q A U H B W G Z T G
  D N E M Y K S W T R O P H Y U
  A Z V G D D E F E A T K A E
  H Q U A L I F I E R X X L Z B
    D A E K U I I G K C W F H C V
    M J L Y H B E U D I X A W E Y Y
    N N E J C X L N X U X Q D G
          C F J C H Z Y H
```

BRILLIANT PLAY. YOU'RE DESTINED FOR GREATNESS!

FOOTBALL QUIZ ANSWERS

1 - Which footballer is often referred to as 'CR7'? - **A) Cristiano Ronaldo**

2 - How many times has Lionel Messi won the Ballon d'Or as of 2024? - **C) 8**

3 - Who is the youngest goalscorer in a World Cup tournament? - **B) Pelé**

4 - Which club holds the record for the longest unbeaten run in the Premier League? - **D) Arsenal**

5 - What do you call a match played between two teams from the same city? - **C) Derby match**

6 - Who won the 2022 FIFA World Cup? - **A) Argentina**

7 - Which player scored the 'Hand of God' goal? - **C) Diego Maradona**

8 - Which club did David Beckham play for after leaving Manchester United? - **A) Real Madrid**

9 - Which national team won the first-ever FIFA World Cup in 1930? - **B) Uruguay**

10 - Who won the Golden Boot at the 2018 FIFA World Cup? - **C) Harry Kane**

11 - Which club is nicknamed 'The Gunners'? - **C) Arsenal FC**

12 - What does VAR stand for in football? - **B) Video Assistant Referee**

13 - Which Italian club has won the most Serie A titles? - **B) Juventus**

14 - What is the nickname of the Italian national football team? - **C) Azzurri**

15 - Which player has scored the fastest hat-trick in Premier League history? - **B) Sadio Mane**

16 - Which footballer was nicknamed 'El Fenómeno'?- **C) Ronaldo Nazário**

17 - Which country won the first Women's World Cup in 1991? - **C) USA**

18 - What is the name of Real Madrid's stadium? - **B) Santiago Bernabéu**

19 - Most goals scored in a single Premier League season (as of 2024)? - **C) Erling Haaland**

20 - What year did England win the FIFA World Cup? - **A) 1966**

21 - Which club did Kylian Mbappé play for before joining Paris Saint-Germain? - **C) AS Monaco**

22 - Which Premier League club is has a 'claret and blue' kit alongside West Ham? - **A) Aston Villa**

23 - What animal is featured on the badge of Leicester City? - **B) Fox**

24 - What is the nickname of Newcastle United? - **A) The Magpies**

WORD UNSCRAMBLE

#1

1 - RAYHR NAKE → HARRY KANE

2 - CLANED ECIR → DECLAN RICE

3 - LEOC PELARM → COLE PALMER

4 - HILP NEDFO → PHIL FODEN

5 - BAYKUO KAAS → BUKAYO SAKA

#2

1 - NELLIO MISSE → LIONEL MESSI

2 - IANLYK BAMPEP → KYLIAN MBAPPE

3 - RINGEL HANDLAA → ERLING HAALAND

4 - ROADNLO → RONALDO

5 - MARYEN → NEYMAR

#3

1 - LANEGND → ENGLAND

2 - BARLIZ → BRAZIL

3 - PANJA → JAPAN

4 - GERINIA → NIGERIA

5 - CERFAN → FRANCE

#4

1 - VENROET → EVERTON

2 - HAMFUL → FULHAM

3 - MANTOETTH → TOTTENHAM

4 - SALECHE → CHELSEA

5 - WETSEANCL → NEWCASTLE

RIDDLES

1 - I protect you from kicks and blows on the field, worn under socks and never revealed. I'm hard on the outside, soft on the skin, keeping your legs safe while you win. What am I?
Answer: **Shin pads**

2 - I wear a special band on my arm, leading my team with strength and charm. I make decisions, guide the play, and inspire the team every match day. Who am I?
Answer: **Captain**

3 - I stretch behind posts to catch what flies through, a target for players to aim and pursue. When I ripple, the crowd may cheer; without me, balls would disappear. What am I?
Answer: **Goal net**

4 - I start and stop the game's flow, a short sharp sound to let players know. In the hands of one who controls the play, my signal can change the course of the day. What am I?
Answer: **Whistle**

CRYPTOGRAM CHALLENGE!
SOLUTIONS

Game 1, Item 1:

PASS **SHOOT**

SCORE!

Game 1, Item 2:

DRIBBLE **TO**

VICTORY!

Game 2, Item 1:

BELIEVE **IN**

YOUR **TEAM**!

Game 2, Item 2:

BACK **OF** **THE**

NET!

Game 3, Item 1:

KEEP **YOUR** **EYE**

ON **THE** **BALL**!

Game 3, Item 2:

GIVE **IT** **YOUR**

BEST **SHOT**!

Game 4, Item 1:

PLAY **LIKE** **A**

CHAMPION!

Game 4, Item 2:

WINNERS **NEVER**

QUIT!

Game 5, Item 1:

FOOTBALL **IS**

LIFE!

Game 5, Item 2:

THE **CROWD**

GOES **WILD**!

CRYPTOGRAM CHALLENGE!
SOLUTIONS

Game 6, Item 1:
ON THE WAY TO
WEMBLEY

Game 6, Item 2:
RISE TO THE
CHALLENGE

Game 7, Item 1:
HEAD IT TO THE
GOAL

Game 7, Item 2:
KICK IT TO
WIN IT

Game 8, Item 1:
DEFEND LIKE A
LION

Game 8, Item 2:
PLAY WITH HEART
AND HUSTLE

Game 9, Item 1:
TRAIN HARD
PLAY HARDER

Game 9, Item 2:
CHASE THE BALL
CHASE THE DREAM

Game 10, Item 1:
SHOOT FOR THE
STARS

Game 10, Item 2:
AIM HIGH
SCORE BIG

Printed in Dunstable, United Kingdom

67236833R00063